A STORY OF
MYSTERY AND ADVENTURE

THE SILVER STAG
of Bunratty

OTHER BOOKS BY EITHNE MASSEY

THE SECRET OF KELLS

About *The Secret of Kells*:
'This was one of the best books I have read
… I would give it 10 out of 10'
EVENING ECHO – reader review

'A rich, exciting and distinctive narrative that
should greatly appeal to young readers,
especially those aged 10+'
INIS

'Eithne Massey has created an exciting
adaptation of the Cartoon Saloon's film'
BOOKS IRELAND

BEST-LOVED IRISH LEGENDS

EITHNE MASSEY is the author of a number of books for children, including *The Secret of Kells, Best-loved Irish Legends, The Dreaming Tree* and *Where the Stones Sing,* and of *Legendary Ireland* for adults. She has had a life-long interest in Irish history and mythology, and now lives between her native town of Dublin and rural Brittany.

THE SILVER STAG

of Bunratty

EITHNE MASSEY

THE O'BRIEN PRESS
DUBLIN

First published 2011 by The O'Brien Press Ltd,
12 Terenure Road East, Rathgar, Dublin 6, Ireland.
Tel: +353 1 4923333; Fax: +353 1 4922777
E-mail: books@obrien.ie
Website: www.obrien.ie

ISBN:978-1-84717-206-8

British Library Cataloguing-in-Publication Data
A catalogue record for this title is available from the British Library

1 2 3 4 5 6 7 8 9 10
11 12 13 14 15

The O'Brien Press receives
assistance from

Editing, typesetting, layout and design: The O'Brien Press Ltd
Cover image courtesy of iStockphoto
Printed and bound by CPI Cox and Wyman Ltd.
The paper used in this book is produced using pulp from managed forests.

CONTENTS

PART I

THE SILVER STAG

CHAPTER 1

THE HOSTAGE

 uan shivered in the cold air. Even though it was dark, he could see that the river had become narrower. The branches of the trees on either side of the boat almost met over his head. Through the web of twigs and small leaves the full moon shone, its light split into a thousand silver pieces. It had been a thin crescent when they had taken him from his home. The familiar smell of water and mud was mixed with something else now. Tuan sniffed. Smoke, maybe? The boat slid under the branches of a blackthorn tree and the petals scattered over him, the thorns scratching his scalp. He bent his head as much as he could, but he could not put up his arms to protect himself because his wrists were tied in front of him and the rope secured around his waist. The Captain of the Guard, Fat John, had done that. Fat John had done it purely to humiliate him. He knew that Tuan would not try to escape.

Tuan raised his head and looked around him as the boat came clear of the trees. Even if he had wanted to escape, he would be completely lost in this strange country of field and river and low-lying lakes, far away from his home in the hills beyond Cratloe Forest. Around him, the landscape was silver, the shapes of the distant hills black.

Something silver flashed across the moonlit field and was gone in an instant. Tuan blinked. Was it some kind of animal? A horse, a deer? Animals were not silver; white or cream, maybe, like the horses in his father's herds, but not silver. Was the colour a trick of the moon or of his tired eyes?

'Look sharp now, we'll need to pull in soon, ye stinking lazy dogs.' Fat John was shouting, as usual.

By now Tuan heartily hated the Captain of the Guard. He was a huge, grossly fat man, wide and red and the owner of several chins, and a rough, red moustache that bristled on a face scarred from many fights. He never spoke without cursing and rarely without shouting. Tuan was careful never to catch his eye; he had been the victim of one too many of his casual, vicious blows.

He wondered if they had finally reached the castle. Please let it be so, he thought. He did not know what to expect there, but nothing could be worse than the past few days. He had lost all sense of time. Life had become a nightmare, each day starting with a kick from one of the soldiers. As soon as he was up, he was bundled onto a mule, his wrists tied and the mule itself attached by a leading rope to the saddle of Fat John. Then, after a long day's march, a meal of hard bread and sour ale eaten around fires that seemed to take forever to light in the cold, damp evenings of late spring.

At first, they had travelled through forest, where no-one cared if the branches whipped his face as they made their way through the trees. At every step, Tuan was afraid he might fall off, more afraid of the shame of it than the pain it would cause him. Then came the boat, the stink of fish and the putrid water at the bottom. He had gagged on it when Fat John had thrown him into it. Fat John looked on, laughing, as the boy struggled to sit upright.

The horses and dogs who accompanied the soldiers had been better treated than Tuan throughout the journey. But then, the animals themselves had treated him better than the soldiers had. He had even made friends with one of the half-grown dogs, a, brown-faced hound with shining, friendly eyes that Fat John referred to as Dumbutt, but Tuan had secretly named Gile, which in his language meant 'brightness'.

The boat travelled from the broad banks of the Shannon into a smaller tributary, and now there was light along the shoreline and voices shouting in English. It was pulled to the left and Tuan was dragged ashore. Through the undergrowth he could see lights high in the sky. It must be a hill, he thought, but as they made their way through the trees, he realised that the lights, so high up, were shining from the castle itself. He stared. He had never seen a building this tall; but then, he had never been so close to a castle. Huge stone walls circled a tower, its whiteness looming over him out of the darkness. Fat John shouted, 'Move on, or I'll have your guts for garters and your livers for breakfast.'

Tuan struggled forward. He had a confused sense of crossing a bridge, of the harsh noise of a metal grid raised to let them in, of a vast doorway – and then he was inside the gates, his eyes blinking in the stinging smoke that came from the rushlights the guards held up to his face.

'So this is the hostage, then,' said one of them.

Fat John grunted and dragged Tuan into a small room

just off the courtyard. He flung the boy inside, his hands still bound, so that he fell onto the floor, almost hitting his face.

'Get in there and keep quiet, or you'll feel my strap,' the Captain of the Guard shouted as he slammed the door behind him.

Be brave, Tuan thought to himself. You are a Mac Conmara. We are the sea-dogs who know no fear. Be brave. He lay there, his head aching, his throat dry from thirst, his misery deepened by the fact that he could feel tears trickling down his face. At least there was no-one to see them.

The room was almost totally bare. He sniffed. The place smelt of pigs, with a faint undertone of chickens. Straw covered the floor, and a wooden bench had been placed under a tiny, barred window high up in the wall, with a pointed top like a church door. No light, except a thin line of moonlight that lit up one corner of the room. Just for a moment he thought he could see two other boys, bound and gagged like him, in the faint glow; but then he blinked and there was no-one there. He stared at that corner until the dawn started to break and a cock started crowing. Tuan felt as if it was crowing directly in his ear. Be brave, he told himself again. He was very tired of being brave. Finally, he managed to curl up on the floor. What he would have liked more than anything else was to be able to cover his face with his bound hands.

He was woken by the noise of the door scraping against the stone floor. Two figures came into the room; one of them was carrying a bundle of clothes and the other a bowl and towels. Light streamed through the open door, blinding the boy.

Both figures were female, but they could not have been more different. The woman carrying the clothes was tall and almost as fat as Fat John; her face was round as a pudding, but she was beaming at him, though after a moment her cheerful look was replaced by a frown.

'What state did that miscreant leave you in, then? And you a guest of my master. Here, girl, help me lift him onto the bench and we'll take off those cords.' She spoke in English.

The smaller figure was a girl of about his own age, or a little younger. She was thin and red-haired and she smiled at him, but said nothing. She set down the bowl she was carrying and helped the large woman shift Tuan onto the seat and untie his wrists. They were raw, bleeding from the rope. He rubbed his eyes and realised that his face was covered in blood from where the blackthorn had scratched him.

'There, my lamb,' said the fat woman, 'Margaret will look after you. Cliar, run to the stills cupboard and fetch some of Dame Anna's green ointment. Here's the key. Hurry now!'

The girl nodded and the woman spent the next few minutes fussing over Tuan, washing his wounds and his face and keeping up a stream of talk that at times Tuan found difficult to follow. His English was good; he had learned it from a boy his own age, a hostage who had stayed with his people for months. But Margaret never stopped to draw breath.

Finally she said, 'And what's your name, lad?'

'I am Tuan, of the Mac Conmara clan of the hills east of the Cratloe woods.' He said it proudly.

Margaret raised her eyebrows. She looked as if she was about to say something, but at that moment the girl came back with the ointment.

'You put it on him, Cliar. You're the one with the healer's touch.'

While the girl smeared the cool, green paste on his wrists, Tuan had the chance to look at her more closely behind her curtain of hair. She was pale-skinned and freckled, like him, but her eyes were not blue like his, but a pale grey-green. She smiled at him shyly, but still said nothing. After the ointment had been rubbed on his wrists, Tuan found that he could move them without pain.

'Thank you,' he said carefully, in English.

'You're welcome,' she replied, in perfect Irish.

Tuan breathed a sigh of relief. At least some people in the castle spoke his language.

Margaret was laying out the clothes she had brought on the bed. 'These look like a good enough fit and will be better than those barbarous rags you're wearing. Now you, boy, get them on and make haste about it; Sir Richard wants to see you and you cannot go to him and his lady looking like a beggar. Come, Cliar, we must organise food for the lad. But eat it quickly, boy.' She paused. 'And just in case you were thinking of trying to escape, don't. The castle is very well guarded.'

'I will not try to escape. It would be against my honour.'

Margaret snorted. 'Honour, indeed! All that kind of talk makes my head ache, and there's far too much of it in this castle. Now, Fat John will be here soon to lead you to His Lordship. But I'll have a word with him before he comes to you, so there will be no more roughness. Captain of the

Guard or not, he'll do as I say if he wants himself and his men to eat well while they're here in Bunratty.'

They left, and Tuan began to struggle into his new clothes. They fitted him well enough, but their bright colours and thin weaves felt strange, so different from the rough, warm wool and soft fur of home. Within a few minutes the young girl had brought him bread and milk. Tuan tried to talk to her, but although she smiled at him shyly, she would not stay. After he had gulped the meal down, he began to feel better. Margaret had annoyed him, but, after all, how could an Englishwoman like Margaret understand the Irish idea of honour that prevented any thought of escape? And at least she had treated him with courtesy, as a guest rather than a prisoner.

For he was not a prisoner. He had not been captured, but sent by his father, to be held hostage by Richard De Clare, Lord of Bunratty. Giving and taking hostages was a way of life in Thomond, indeed all over the island of Ireland and beyond. As long as he was held by Sir Richard, he was the guarantee that his father's people would not attack the castle or the lands surrounding it. As long as they kept the peace, he would be treated well. But if his father's branch of the Mac Conmaras – McNamaras, as they were now sometimes called – went to war against the English, things would be very different for him. He would certainly be maimed, losing an eye or an ear. He might even be killed.

CHAPTER 2

RICHARD DE CLARE

Whatever Margaret had said to Fat John, it certainly worked, for when he returned, he led Tuan down to the Great Hall without tying him up again, though he said nothing and looked sulky, spitting on the floor as he opened the door to the hall.

Tuan gasped as he went through the doorway. The Great Hall was huge – bigger than the abbey church in Quin, the largest, highest place he had ever seen. Like the abbey church, as soon as you entered your eyes were drawn to the wall opposite the door. But here, instead of an altar, there was a great fireplace. Seated in front of it, at a table covered with food, were a harsh-faced man and a thin-faced woman, the woman holding a small child, who wriggled on her lap. So this was Sir Richard De Clare and his wife, the Lady

Johanna. Tuan had heard all about them. All of them, it seemed, were more intent on their trenchers of food than in paying any attention to the boy who was slowly making his way towards their table.

This gave Tuan the chance to look around him. There was a fire burning in the huge hearth and there seemed to be a chimney, so the room was clear of the smoke that filled most halls; Tuan had never seen a chimney before. The room was filled with trestle tables and benches, now mostly empty. Servants were dismantling them and standing them up against the walls. A few soldiers still sat astride the benches, spearing their food with their knives, while dogs sniffed around the floor for the morsels they dropped. The walls had been whitewashed with lime and they were covered with trophies of the kill – the heads of boars and wolves, huge antlers from the forest stags. On one wall there was what seemed to be a tapestry, showing a hunt in the forest, men in bright clothes with horns and hounds, all surrounded by green leaves. It looked real and yet not real; the birds in the branches were too still, the flowers that covered the forest floor were too bright and stiff. Tuan's scrutiny was interrupted by a cool voice. It came from Sir Richard.

'So, you are Sorley Mac Conmara's boy! A small enough surety, I see.' He laughed at his own joke, and there was a polite titter from the others around the room.

'Well, boy, you are a guest here for as long as your father holds faith with us. And you will be treated as such. Matthieu here is only a couple of years younger than you. He is my ward. He will look after you and you will attend lessons with him.'

Sir Richard paused, his eye lighting on a small, round-faced boy seated near him. 'Matthieu, come over and greet the boy. You will show him the castle and where he needs to go. And tell Margaret to fit him out with whatever he needs. I am glad to see that he has already been given some civilised clothing.'

The chubby-faced boy scrambled down off his bench and came towards Tuan. As he came close, Tuan saw that he was smiling. He looked nice, with his fair hair cut in a slightly crooked fringe over his forehead and wide blue eyes. For a horrible moment, Tuan thought he was going to kiss him on the cheek but then, with a glance at De Clare, the boy seemed to decide against it. Instead, he took Tuan's hand, as if to lead him away. But Tuan had suddenly remembered the lesson impressed upon him by his own father and mother. These people might be barbarians, but that did not mean that the son of Sorley Mac Conmara and Sive O'Dea had to act like one. He shook off Matthieu's hand and made a deep bow, Norman fashion, saying in his best English:

'While I am in your house I am yours to command, my lord and lady.'

Sir Richard merely nodded. There was no expression on his face, with its long, thin nose and narrow lips, its heavy eyelids over dark eyes that seemed strangely blank. This man was older than Tuan's father, and his reputation, that of Claraghmore, the Great De Clare, was known all over Thomond and far beyond. Tuan's mother, trying hard not to cry, had told him all about the Lord of Bunratty. He had become lord of the castle when he was very young, for his father had died when he was a child and his elder brother, Gilbert, had only been lord for a short time before he too had died. Despite his youth, Sir Richard had held onto power in a part of the world where only the very strongest and wiliest survived. Even Tuan's people spoke of him with awe, for no-one could deny that he was a great warrior and a dangerously clever enemy.

But now the Lady Johanna spoke for the first time. She

was pale and thin and Tuan could glimpse blond hair under her headdress. Her clothes were very rich and fine, but her face was too stiff and her eyes set too close together for beauty. She spoke in English.

'Indeed, it has vastly pretty manners for a savage! Perhaps, Maude, you could take a lesson from the wild Irish. Be sure to watch his ways.' She gave a sneering laugh, and the child on her lap giggled too.

The dark-eyed girl she had addressed scowled, then shrugged her shoulders and gave Tuan a filthy look. At first he thought she was not going to bother to reply, but then she said, in English too but with an accent very different from the Lady Johanna's: 'I might as well to take lessons from the Irish wolfhounds that fight with each other around the fire, my lady. Did you hear that jest about the one that was chewing a bone and then stood up and walked away on three legs?'

Tuan drew a sharp breath. But Matthieu was pulling his arm urgently, and he allowed himself to be led from the Great Hall.

Once outside, Matthieu let go of his arm and said apologetically: 'Don't pay any heed to my sister; she never misses the chance to be rude to Lady Johanna. They can't stand each other. She didn't mean anything against you, you know.'

The boy spoke in English, but with an accent like his sister's, an accent Tuan could not place. It was not Irish, that was for sure, nor straightforward English like Margaret's. Nor was it the strange crossbreed accent that the Norman-English lords and ladies spoke, though that was the closest to it.

'You are not English, are you?' he asked Matthieu.

Matthieu shook his head. 'No – and don't let Maude hear you suggest that we are! I do not know quite what we are.' He smiled. 'Normans, mostly, I suppose. My family was a crusading one. You have heard of the Crusades?'

Tuan nodded. Everyone knew of the great armies that had been sent to the east to claim Jerusalem for the Christians of Europe.

'Well, my great grandfather was a Frank, but he went to Jerusalem, to fight for the holy city. I don't remember Outremer at all, but Maude sometimes tells me stories about it. I don't think she can really remember it either, but our mother talked to her about what it was like there. My grandfather settled down there, and began trading. Then, after the Mamluks took over, we had to go away. We came westwards. We went to Italy, and then to France. My father is a soldier, so he has always worked for whatever army would take him on – though he only works for the most noble of lords. We always went with him, until Maman died. My mother refused to be left waiting and worrying as to what might happen to him and always travelled along with him. But in the end it was not my father who died, but Maman. She got sick in Antwerp. My father said it was the cold did it.'

He stopped for a moment, drew breath and continued. 'We were sent away. We went to England first, to cousins. But then we did something that got us into trouble, even though the person we did it to deserved it – and so we were sent over here. Sir Richard is only some kind of distant relative, so Lady Johanna says that it was really very good of her to take us in at all. But she and Maude don't like each other, so it's difficult. And now, if we are thrown out of here, there is really nowhere else for us to go after Bunratty. We have gone as far west as we can, unless we sail out into the western ocean and fall off the edge of the world.' He laughed, but his voice shook.

Tuan got the feeling that he had made up the joke to hide his fear. It must be frightening, he thought, to know that you had no real home.

'What about your father?' he asked.

Matthieu shrugged. 'Our father left us to fight with the Hospitaller Knights in Rhodes, and promised to come to fetch us as soon as he could. But that was over a year ago and there has been no word from him. It seems that he might be—' He stopped and swallowed.

Then he said: 'Look, this is the room where Maude and I sleep.'

They had been climbing up stairs and had now reached the door of a room in a side tower, and the boy was breathless. He opened the door and Tuan peered into the room. He had heard that the English had strange curtained things called beds, but there were none in here, just two straw pallets on the floor, a table with a jug and basin, a couple of wooden chests and a peg where a brown and a blue cloak hung side by side. The shutters of the narrow window were open and the air smelt much fresher than in his little room. Matthieu went over to one of the chests, and lifted the lid.

'Come and see my treasures,' he said. But he was interrupted. The dark-haired girl, Maude, was glaring at them from the door.

✳ ✳ ✳

So, thought Maude as she looked at the two boys, now, on top of everything else, it looked as if Matthieu was making friends with the Irish hostage. He would desert her and she would have no-one. She would be even more lonely for Outremer and their past life. There were nights when Maude dreamed that she was back in Outremer, and woke up with tears on her face, which she would quickly wipe away so no-one would see that she was crying. How she missed being there! How she missed the sun – ever since she and Matthieu had arrived in Bunratty there had hardly been a sight of it, nothing but rain and mist.

Maude was old enough to remember Outremer, though very faintly. Sometimes she wondered if the pictures in her mind were real memories or just her imagination, because the stories her mother had told her about living in the east were so very vivid in her mind. There were times when something very small could bring it all back to her. The smell of spices in the kitchen could do it. Suddenly she would be back there, she would see the colours, feel the heat on her skin, smell the scents that she had not realised meant home to her: cardamom and clove, ginger and nutmeg, grains of paradise and cinnamon and mace. Other smells meant home too – the rough leather of her father's saddle and jerkin, when he would pull her up onto his horse and take her on one of his wild gallops through the desert. She would never forget those gallops, the hot sun on their faces, the warmth of the wind tangling her hair so that her mother would pretend to be angry when her father brought her back home. Her mother would laugh then, and bathe her face in rosewater.

The warmth was part of being with her father, Sir Baldwin. When he had ridden away to fight against the Turks, he had told her to be brave and to take care of Matthieu. But it had been hard. In England they had been moved around their distant relatives like unwanted puppies, and finally ended up in the far north, in the household of Lady Margaret de Baddlesmere. Lady Margaret had not really paid much heed to them at all, which suited Maude quite well, for it meant that she was able to spend all her time practising archery with the soldiers of the castle. But then there had been the incident with a visiting squire, a horrible boy who had ill-treated his horse and had, in Maude's view, richly deserved his punishment. He had ended up in the horse trough, the result of a well-deserved push from behind, jointly administered by Maude and Matthieu. But the result of *that* had been total disgrace. They had been shipped over to Ireland, to Lady

Margaret's brother, Richard. Maude had wondered why Lady Margaret had raised her eyebrows when she heard that Lady Johanna had agreed to take in the children. It was only when they arrived that Maude realised that Lady Johanna had wanted her as a nursemaid for baby Thomas and as lady-in-waiting for herself. All Lady Johanna's other companions had deserted her because of her vicious temper and the discomforts of living in a draughty castle, in a state of almost perpetual warfare with the wild Irish.

But in Maude, Lady Johanna had met her match. The lady-in-waiting and, indeed, the nursemaid plans were abandoned very early on. But Maude's rebelliousness had not made life easy for her and she hated Bunratty. She had nearly gone mad during the winter, trapped between the walls of the castle. But at least Bunratty *was* a castle, with proper stone walls; she had heard such terrible stories about Ireland before she came over that she had been afraid that everyone lived in mud huts like the peasants in Outremer. The peasants here lived in mud huts too, with thatched roofs, and pigs scrambling through them and sharing their quarters with their owners. That was, no doubt, the kind of place the Irish boy came from, though he called himself the son of a chief and seemed proud enough to be one.

Now she said to her brother: 'Are you going to spend all day with the Irish wolfhound?' She did not look in Tuan's direction. 'I want you to come and practise shooting with me. Myles has set up the target on the roof.'

Matthieu smiled, and said to Tuan: 'My sister, Maude, is the best shot in Bunratty, so I don't know why she wants *me* to practise with her. I'm hopeless. But would you like to come with us? I'm sure Myles will be able to find a bow and arrow for you.'

'So he can shoot us dead and escape?' said Maude scornfully, at last turning to Tuan.

'I would not do such a thing,' said Tuan angrily. 'I have agreed to come here of my own free will to act as a surety for my people. If I escape it will break the truce. I would not want to be the cause of warfare.'

'Another dove of peace!' said the girl scornfully. 'As if there weren't enough pigeons in the castle already.' As she said this, one fluttered in from outside. It sat on the window-sill and looked in at her, its head to one side. She made a face at it and it flew away.

'I'm not afraid of battle,' said Tuan. 'I'll challenge any knight you dare to put against me at shooting the bow or in hand-to-hand combat.'

The girl looked at him closely and then she smiled. A small, pleased smile.

'Very well, we may just do that,' she said. 'But not today. Today is for fun. Come on, you two! Last one to reach the tower roof smells like Fat John!'

CHAPTER 3

THE KITCHEN MAID

 liar was working in the kitchen, a vast, cavernous place. Most of the servants worked here, as it took a great deal of people to keep everyone in the castle fed. The long tables were piled with food of all kinds. The kitchen smelt of a hundred different things – woodsmoke and roasting meat and raw fish and spices – and was always full of noise and bustle.

Cliar's tasks included everything from fetching water to strewing and clearing the rushes that covered the floor, from stirring the vast pots of soup and stew that were hung over the open fireplaces to helping the kitchen boys who turned the spits. If she was lucky, she might be asked to help with grating sugar from a sugar loaf and mixing it with almonds to make sweet marchpane.

This morning her job was to help Margaret knead the dough for the next day's bread. Once the dough was kneaded, it would be let sit for hours, before being baked in the great ovens that almost filled one wall. Vast quantities of bread were baked every night, for the castle was home to a standing army, soldiers who patrolled Sir Richard's lands to keep them free of the Irish clans.

Kneading the dough was hard work, but Cliar liked it. It left plenty of time for talk, and it was always warm in the kitchen. The work was certainly better than the endless chopping of vegetables that was one of her main tasks, or the even more endless scrubbing of floors. Cliar could not remember a time when her hands had not been raw and sore from her work in the kitchen. Sometimes Margaret gave her some pig grease to put on them and sometimes the lady in the north west tower gave her sweetly scented ointment, which worked far better than Margaret's lard. But most of the time Cliar's hands were covered in blisters from water and the harsh soap that she herself helped to make from wood ash and lye. At soap-making they sang to keep their spirits up, but at bread-making Margaret told stories or exchanged gossip with the other servants. The heat and the exertion seemed to make Margaret say more than she usually did, which was quite a lot.

Today Margaret was on one of her rants against Lady Johanna. As always, Cliar wished that her old friend would learn to keep her voice down, for there were those in the castle who might report what she said to Lady Johanna herself. Many of those who worked in Bunratty had come over from England with Richard De Clare's lady and owed their first loyalty to her. But even if they were loyal to her ladyship, no-one could be said to love her. It was hard to love the Lady Johanna, with her nose forever twitching its way into other people's business and her merciless punishment of anything she considered below her standards. The fact that her standards changed according to her mood didn't help matters at all.

'The old stoat has me bothered with her complaints about the linen,' Margaret grumbled. 'It can never be white enough nor smell sweet enough for her. And it's hard enough to keep it clean at all without a good day's drying since Easter. What a spring! More like November, April was!'

'Never mind Easter! There's hardly been a good day's drying this past year,' agreed Janet, who was passing by carrying half a dozen rabbits by the ears. 'If it's a bad summer, I think we may all give up hope. The harvest of last year could not have fed an ordinary household, much less Sir Richard's army.'

'It's this cursed, endless rain.' Margaret threw her eyes up to heaven. 'I hear it's worse in other parts, though, and that there are people leaving their children in the forest because they can't feed them. The poor things end up eaten by wolves, like as not.'

'And there are worse things than wolves in the forests now – men that eat children, they say!' Janet shivered. 'There are gangs hiding there that are more savage than the wild animals themselves. I don't know how you have the nerve to go there to gather Dame Anna's plants, Cliar. I'd be terrified.'

Cliar smiled. She loved her days in the forest. But nobody in the kitchen seemed to understand that. 'It's in the forests south of the Shannon that the wild men are, they say, not up here. And at least now we are nearly at the end of the hungry months,' she said.

'And there's to be a hunt soon,' said Janet. 'I heard the master of hounds say so when I fetched these rabbits. That will mean venison for the larder. Did you hear that the Silver Stag has been seen?'

Margaret stopped her kneading. 'I did not, then. That's a sign of death, they say.'

'Oh nonsense,' Janet laughed. 'If they catch it, it will be a sign of food for weeks to come!'

Young Marcus, who was supposed to be minding the spit, called over: 'Is it really true that the stag is pure silver?'

Margaret lowered her voice to a whisper. 'It is. It's seen by moonlight, in the forest, and its body is like the moon itself and its great antlers shine like the silver cups on the lord's table.' Marcus looked scared.

Allison, who had been listening to the talk without saying anything, snorted. She was one of the English who had come to Bunratty with Lady Johanna and she looked down on the superstitions of the local people. 'Old women's stories! I warrant it was seen by someone who had too much of Lord De Clare's good wine!'

Margaret shook her head. She too was English, but she had lived in Bunratty too long to dismiss the strange stories that were told about the castle and the lands around it.

'If the stag has been seen, it is surely a sign that something important is going to happen,' she declared. 'Great change will come to Bunratty. Mark my words!'

She turned to Cliar. 'Why child, you're as pale as a ghost. Are you not well?'

Cliar shook her head. She couldn't speak.

'Well, I'll finish up here. It's nearly done anyway. Get you up to Dame Anna and ask her for a posset. I cannot have you sick tonight. Kate and Matty are both sick already and the rest of us will be needed to serve in the Great Hall. Hurry on, now.'

Cliar moved away from the table as quickly and quietly as she could. Over the years she had learned to move like a cat, unseen; it helped avoid trouble. But now she moved with a purpose. She had to tell this news to Dame Anna as soon as possible.

CHAPTER 4

FAT JOHN

s she made her way to the north west tower, Cliar felt her stomach start to settle. Dame Anna would know what to do. She'd thought she was going to be sick when they had started talking about hunting the Silver Stag. She had never told anyone, but once, coming home late in the snow on a winter's evening from a plant collecting expedition, she had seen him. He was standing with his head raised high in the woods to the north of Bunratty. His antlers were shining against the night sky and the frosted branches of the trees, his figure etched in moonlight and starlight. She had never seen anything so beautiful; he seemed so free, so far away from the noise and dirt of Cliar's daily life in the Bunratty kitchens. She had gazed in awe at the magnificent creature. The thought of him brought down by dogs and arrows, cut to pieces to become gobbets of meat for the table was unbearable.

Cliar was sure that Dame Anna would be able to help; she was wise and knew things that other people, even Margaret, did not. Margaret was clever and kind, but she could do nothing to change the ways of Bunratty. Dame Anna was not especially kind, indeed she was somewhat frightening, but she was powerful. She seemed to know so much, though she never left her tower and she often refused to share her knowledge. Deep inside, Cliar also felt that Dame Anna knew something about Cliar's own life before she had come to Bunratty. Margaret said that it was impossible that Cliar herself could remember anything about her early life, for she had been found as a tiny child, left in a straw cradle at the gates of the castle. But sometimes, in her dreams, she heard a soft voice singing – why was there the sense of a woman, a woman with coils of long red hair that Cliar would lift her hand to, to pull and play with? And why did she remember the laugh that would follow, and a man's voice, deep and gentle, with laughter in it too?

Cliar, the kitchen women had called her, after the wisps of straw carried by young girls at Lughnasa. She had been found at Lughnasa, that day at the end of July when young girls carried those burning wisps up to the top of the hill at Lough Gur, the magical lake to the south of Bunratty. This was done in honour of the god Lugh and the goddess Áine, Lord and Lady of the Harvest. Cliar sometimes wondered what her real name was and who her mother and father might have been. She knew they could not be alive, for she was sure that the red-haired woman would never have left her by choice. But somewhere, perhaps, she had cousins and kin, a family who would give her a place in the world. It seemed that everyone else had one. The Irish hostage, Tuan, might be far from his family, Matthieu and Maude might be orphans, but at least they all knew who their people were. Even the ghosts of the castle had a place, and knew their kin.

What was her place? Up to a year ago it had been in the kitchen, running errands for Margaret and listening to her complain. But then everything had changed. Then she had met Dame Anna. From the time Cliar was tiny, she had heard stories of the lady in the north west tower, and had seen the servants delivering flax and fleece to the door at the bottom of the staircase. No-one ever saw the lady come to collect it, but the next day it would be gone. A few weeks later the servants would find linen and woollen cloth, finely spun and woven, left in bundles outside that same doorway. Food and drink were left in the same way. Indeed, Cliar herself had sometimes been the one sent to do so, leaving the food beside the strange figure carved in the stone by the doorway, and collecting the scraps and used dishes afterwards. Once or twice, crossing the courtyard, she had caught a glimpse of a figure in the window of the tower. But no-one, not even Margaret, would talk to her about Dame Anna. Dame Anna spun and wove and made medicines for the castle, but she was never seen. From the window of her tower, birds flew in and out constantly: a flock of grey pigeons and two strange birds – a black dove and a great white owl.

Then, one day Cliar found an abandoned kitten, left to die behind the waste heap where she had gone in the early morning with the ashes from the kitchen fires. She was just in time to save it from Wolf, one of Fat John's favourite hounds, a malicious beast that possessed an appetite as large as its master's and a character just as unpleasant. She lifted the tiny kitten up, felt its heart beating faintly in the palm of her hand, and looked into the eyes that were just beginning to open to a milky blue. One of its legs was dangling, broken. Cliar had a basic knowledge of medicine and she splinted the broken leg. She kept the kitten hidden in a box in an alcove in the barn, well away from the castle cats and dogs. She told nobody about the sick kitten. She knew that the only solution she would be offered was a sack and a stone and the river. Despite her careful feeding and nursing, however, the kitten was weakening and the leg did not seem to be healing. After a few days she realised that there was only one person who could help her.

Dame Anna had medicines that could cure the most dreadful illnesses, heal the deepest wounds. But the kitchen gossips had filled Cliar with horror stories about the lady in the tower: she was a witch with no back; she had iron teeth and red eyes; she had no nose but a bird's beak; she would turn Cliar into a toad as soon as look at her. Even Cliar's special friends, the castle ghosts, were frightened of Dame Anna, and had gibbered in a frantic manner when they realised what Cliar planned to do.

It had taken all her courage to take the kitten and push open the door of the tower, to walk alone into the musty darkness, to climb the narrow, twisting, forbidden stairs to the lady's room at the top, the kitten mewing faintly in her arms. Looking at the little creature – seeing how near it was to death – was the only thing that gave her courage to continue.

But as soon as she pushed open the door at the top of the tower, she walked into a place of light and birdsong, and the ancient lady seated by her spinning-wheel looked up and smiled at her.

'I have been waiting for you for a long time, Cliar,' she said.

Dame Anna took the kitten gently from her and showed Cliar where his leg had become infected. She told her that the only thing to do was to amputate it so the infection would not spread. They did it together, after putting the kitten to sleep with one of Dame Anna's potions, and Cliar managed to help Dame Anna without fainting or getting sick, though it had been very hard to watch the surgery.

After it was all over, the old lady smiled and said: 'He will be fine when he wakes up, and will soon learn to walk on three legs. As for you, you have a strong stomach and a gift for healing. You must come and help me. I will teach you how to use your gifts.'

The kitten had indeed healed quickly, and the lack of a fourth leg did not stop him from becoming one of the champion mousers of the kitchen. And from then on, Cliar was called to the tower to help Dame Anna and to gather the plants she needed for her potions.

※ ※ ※

Now she moved as quickly as she could across the bailey to where the western stairway led to Dame Anna's tower to tell her of the threat to the Silver Stag. But suddenly she froze. There was a scurrying of feet and barking and shouting, and a group of people came rushing into the yard. Her stomach suddenly flipped over, for she heard the voice that never failed to make her feel faint and sick, to want to run away as fast as she could.

'Give me that dog!' Fat John was shouting. 'If that little runt of a mongrel cannot learn to obey I'll break his legs for him first and then drown him in the Ratty!'

Tuan, Maude and Matthieu were running as fast as they could, pursued by Fat John, who was cursing violently as he ran. A half-grown, panting dog ran with them, barking excitedly as if he thought this was all a game.

'I will not!' Maude turned and shouted back at him. 'You were cruel to him! He's only little and he was terrified! How dare you do that to him!'

'Why not?' said Fat John, with a sneer in his voice. 'It's only some mongrel, and mongrels do not deserve to live unless they learn to know their masters.' He gave Maude a nasty look. 'Do you know your master?'

'I shall tell my guardian!' Maude kept her back straight and was trying hard to control the quiver in her voice. 'He will punish you.'

'For the death of a half-breed dog? I think not, my little lady.'

Tuan joined in. 'It's a barbarous way to treat an animal! If you don't want it, let us keep the dog.'

Matthieu also joined in, his voice shaking but courageous: 'You're nothing but a big fat bully! Leave him alone!'

Fat John blocked the doorway to the hall, a smile on his face. 'I've trapped you now, my pigeons. You have nowhere else to go. Hand over that dog or I'll come over and get it from you!'

The children looked around desperately.

Cliar had no time to think. 'Come,' she said to them, 'Come quickly.' She ran to the small door in the wall of the north west tower, and pushed it open, hustling them in before her. She had only a moment to catch a glimpse of Fat John's outraged expression before she slammed the door in his face.

CHAPTER 5

THE LADY IN THE TOWER

rowded into the small space at the bottom of the stairs, the four children peered at each other through the darkness. The dog, now held tightly in Maude's arms, tried to wriggle out of her grasp and started to lick Cliar's hand as if he knew she was responsible for his rescue.

Maude cuddled him. She was still in a state of shock from what she had seen – Fat John dangling the puppy over the battlements of the castle, beating it with a stick and shouting curses at it. The poor creature had been whimpering and wriggling in his grasp, in terror for its life. She had not thought twice, but raced over and hung out of Fat John's arm, biting it hard. He dropped the puppy and for a terrible moment Maude thought the little creature had fallen from the tower, but instead the dog jumped onto the floor, where he scampered out of Fat John's reach. Maude grabbed him and raced away, almost colliding with Matthieu as he came out of the small trapdoor that led to the roof.

After that everything had happened very quickly. Tuan, following close behind Maude, had seen what was happening and dived at Fat John's ankles, knocking him off balance so that he fell onto the slippery stone surface of the tower. Fat John grabbed at Tuan, but the boy was too quick for him and he too made it down through the door before the Captain of the Guard could get up. The children and the dog raced to the bottom of the stairs, with Fat John grunting angrily behind them. At the base they slammed the door shut and shot the bolts, pausing only a moment to grin at each other before they fled, leaving Fat John roaring in rage to be let out. Unfortunately, one of the soldiers was passing and heard the captain's curses, so they only had the advantage of a few moments before he was in pursuit of them again. Maude led them out into the bailey, hoping that Sir Richard might be there and they could put their case to him. But the bailey was empty except for Cliar.

❋ ❋ ❋

Now the four of them leaned their weight against the door. There was no bolt on this side and they all knew it was only a matter of time before Fat John would manage to push it open. They could hear him grunting and puffing on the other side.

'Ye cursed pool of cat's vomit! Ye devil's spawn! Ye'll all be sorry when I get ye, especially you, witch child, with yer red hair and yer sneaking ways–'

Then there was a sudden silence. The children stared at each other, hardly daring to breathe. Tuan put his finger to his lips. Perhaps Fat John was keeping silent so that they would think he had left and open the door? But as the silence continued Cliar shook her head and Gile – for that was the puppy they had rescued – stopped whimpering.

'He's gone,' she whispered. 'He smells terrible, and now the smell has gone. He's given up.'

'So it's safe to go out? Will we open the door?' Tuan looked around, and they all nodded.

He lifted the latch and pulled. The door was jammed shut. Even with the four of them pulling as hard as they could, the door would still not open.

'He must have jammed the latch with something,' said Maude.

'I didn't hear him do anything,' said Tuan.

'Does it matter?' said Matthieu dolefully. 'Whatever he did, we're stuck in here until he lets us out.'

'Unless we see what's in the tower,' said Tuan. 'Maybe there's another way out.' He looked up where the spiral staircase led upwards into the gloom.

Cliar shook her head. 'This staircase leads to Dame Anna's chamber,' she said. 'There's no other way out.'

'The witch's chamber?' Matthieu's voice was no more than a squeak. 'They say she eats children and sucks their bones!'

'That's rubbish!' said Cliar. 'She's a healer and a wise woman and she knows lots of things. She won't do you any harm.' Her voice trailed off. She was not quite sure if Dame Anna would welcome uninvited strangers into her tower.

'Well, we really don't have a choice,' said Tuan. 'Let's go on up the stairs. I'll lead the way, if you like.'

'No,' said Cliar. 'I'll go first. She knows me.'

Tuan stood back to let her lead. Maude followed, then the boys. They began the long ascent; round and round they went, growing dizzy from the climb. Through the narrow, slitted windows they could catch glimpses of the fields and woods around Bunratty.

'You have been here before?' Tuan called up to Cliar.

'Yes, lots of times. Dame Anna needs plants from the river meadows and the forests to make her cures and simples. She tells me what she wants and I gather them for her. She has even shown me how to make some of her potions.'

'So she *is* a witch! And you, you're a friend of hers ... Fat John called you "witch child"! I suppose I'd better be nice to you or you'll turn me into some kind of horrible beast?' said Tuan, grinning.

'You won't have far to turn,' muttered Maude, and Tuan grabbed the thick, dark plait that hung down her back and pulled it hard.

'I heard that!' he said. 'What makes you think you're so much better than me, anyway?'

'The fact that I'm a pure-blood Norman and you are an Irish savage,' said Maude coolly, pulling her hair free.

'Sssh!' said Cliar. 'We're nearly there. I can hear the spinning wheel.'

They all went silent and listened to a soft, humming sound. The hairs on the back of Maude's neck were beginning to rise. She wondered where the kitchen maid – whom she had often seen but never before spoken to – was leading them. There was a strange, sweet smell that seemed to be coming to meet them on the stairs. It reminded Maude of the incense the priests used in the church and that her nurse in the east had burned to put them to sleep when they were babies. Now there was another noise, the soft murmur of doves and pigeons. They had reached the top of the stairs and before them was a door with the faint silvery sheen of old birchwood. Cliar stopped and raised her hand, but before she had time to knock, the door swung open gently.

✳ ✳ ✳

As Cliar led the way in, the three other children gasped. They had never seen anything like the room they had entered. It was a round room, with windows on all sides, all of them open so that the many birds could fly in and out freely. There were curved wooden shelves against one wall, covered in bottles of all colours – blue and green and red and purple and yellow. On a table there was a single blue bottle and a silver basin filled with water. In the centre of the room there was a fire, golden and burning brightly. It was only afterwards that Maude realised what an odd fire it was, for no smoke came from it.

Seated by the fire was a white-haired woman, with piercing, dark eyes. Her face was white too, and finely wrinkled, as if she were very old. But when she stood up to greet them her back was as straight as a young girl's and she moved as gracefully as a dancer. She was dressed in a black gown, and over her shoulders hung a cloak as white as milk. It seemed to catch the light as she moved, so that when she stood up, the children's eyes were dazzled.

'Welcome, children,' she said.

Cliar went to her and began, 'I'm sorry, Dame Anna, there was nothing—'

The lady put her hand gently to Cliar's cheek. 'Hush, child, there is no need to explain. I saw that you would come to me.'

Then she turned to Tuan and placed her hand on his head. 'Welcome, Tuan, of the clan Mac Conmara. Your people are good people and you are a worthy child of them. And come to me, you two children of the Normans. Let me look at you.'

Maude and Matthieu came over to her. She took Maude's shoulders in her hands so that she was looking directly into her face. 'A brave girl, and proud. But do not be too proud, Maude FitzHerbert, to ask your friends for help.'

Then she lifted Matthieu's chin and looked closely at him. 'You are ashamed because you have not the bright, clear courage of your sister. But do not forget that you have your own kind of valour, and your own kind of strength. When you find that, you will know that you can do wonderful things.'

Cliar was standing slightly to one side, and Dame Anna smiled at her. 'As for you, my helper, you are, I think, already on the path of finding what you will become. Now, all of you, you must sit with me for a while.'

The children noticed that four stools were already placed close to the woman. They sat down, with Gile stretched at Maude's feet, apparently already recovered from his ordeal.

Cliar suddenly remembered why she had wanted to see Dame Anna in the first place. 'It is the stag, Dame Anna, the Silver Stag. It has been sighted and they say there will be a hunt to catch it.'

Dame Anna was silent for a long time.

'So the stag has been seen,' she sighed finally. 'That may mean the end of Bunratty as we know it.'

'Tell us about the stag, is it magic?' Cliar swallowed nervously as she said the word 'magic'. She knew that Dame Anna herself had magical powers, but the word was never used when Cliar worked with her.

'Magic? You might say so. Or you might not. But first,

let me give you some water. You are all looking hot and tired from the chase.'

She went to the shelves and took down four goblets – red, green, blue and yellow. She filled them with water from a silver jug and handed them to the children. Tuan held his yellow glass nervously; he had never drunk from glass before, and he had heard it was very delicate. At home there were pottery and wooden vessels, and sometimes pewter or silver for great festivals, but nothing like this. Being able to see what you were drinking seemed like a kind of magic to him. He held it up to the light; the glass coloured the water a delicate gold.

Dame Anna was speaking in a low, musical voice. 'The stag is part of Tradree – that is the old name for Bunratty. Tradree means 'the strand of the two kings', and one of those kings sometimes takes the form of the stag. For centuries it has appeared at a time when the land is to undergo great change – it was sighted when the first Normans came here, and again when Thomas De Clare died. But it also appears when there is treachery in the air: when the two Mac Conmara hostages were hanged here, two young boys unjustly killed; it was seen when Sir Richard's father, old Thomas, betrayed the friendship of Brian Rua O'Brien and had him treacherously murdered though he was a guest within the walls of Bunratty. The stag is part of Bunratty, and in its blood flows the life of the land. It must not be hunted, it must not be harmed. You must not let the stag be killed. Cliar, you and your young friends must stop it.'

'What friends?' asked Cliar.

'Why, you and Tuan and the young Normans.'

Cliar made a face. 'I don't know if the Normans are my friends.' She looked doubtfully at Maude and Matthieu. Maude stuck her tongue out at her. There was proof, thought Cliar: Maude was hard going. And Matthieu was really just a baby.

'Yes, they are, you just do not realise it yet. And nor do they; but they will. Do not argue or doubt, Cliar. For the tasks that need to be done, the skills of all four of you will be needed. You cannot do what is necessary by yourself.'

'But what can *we* do?' asked Tuan. 'We can't stop the hunt.'

Suddenly, the lady's eyes were turned on him and Tuan felt them burning into his soul.

'I think you can,' said the lady. 'You must use your best skills and ingenuity. If you don't, there will be such doom on this castle and the people in it for generations to come that the grief and shame of those who live here will know no bounds.'

The children were silent. This was suddenly very serious.

'Can't you help us?' asked Matthieu.

'You must find your own path to saving the stag. All I will say is that you – all of you together – can do it. You must all start to think about what I have said and make your plans. You are safe to go down now, for Fat John has left and you can open the door. But keep the dog out of his sight.'

'I'll keep him in my chamber and call him Baskerville, after my father's family lands in England,' said Maude.

'I've already named him Gile,' said Tuan. 'Look, he answers to it.' Gile had pricked up his ears and started to wag his tail when Tuan said his name.

'What does Gile mean?' asked Maude.

'It means "brightness",' said Tuan, 'but to be honest, he's not all that bright.'

Matthieu added, 'But it also sounds like the Irish word, *giolla*, which means "follower", or "friend", or sometimes "young servant", doesn't it?'

'How on earth do you know that?' asked Maude, but not waiting for an answer, continued: 'Bright Follower, I like that. Gile he shall be.'

As they made their way down from the tower, the children were silent. It was all very well for Dame Anna to send them out on this mission to save the stag, but how on earth were they to achieve it? Tuan wondered what he could come up with and decided to go to his room and think hard. Matthieu knew that Maude would make the real plan, whatever he thought of, but he decided to learn as much as he could about hunting anyway in the short time available to him.

Cliar looked at her companions, but said nothing. She already had the germ of an idea in her head. But it would mean that she would have to tell these children her secret. She didn't know if she was ready to do that.

Maude was also thinking furiously. Perhaps they could get something into the horses' or dogs' food on the day of the hunt, just to make them ill enough so that they could not go out? Perhaps they themselves could drive the Silver Stag far from Bunratty? Perhaps she could trip Sir Richard up and sprain his ankle or something? The hunt would certainly not go ahead without him. But each plan seemed more impossible to carry out than the last – and she really didn't see how a kitchen girl, an Irish savage and her own little brother could be of any help at all.

CHAPTER 6

MAUDE AND MATTHIEU

'Really, I don't know how you manage to turn everything you wear into a rag. Matthieu keeps his clothes much better than you do.'

Margaret was fussing around in their room before dinner that evening, pulling out clothes from Maude's chest and clucking over the state of her dresses, while Maude lay stretched on her pallet. Gile was lying across her stomach and snoring, paws in the air and dribbling slightly with pleasure.

'That's because he doesn't do anything. He is the nearest thing to a dormouse I have ever seen. Except that they probably move around more,' said Maude, scratching Gile's stomach gently. Matthieu stuck his tongue out at her. He was drawing Gile, using a piece of grey slate and some charred wood from the fire. Maude had to admit that he was really good at drawing. He had caught Gile's brainless expression perfectly.

Margaret sighed. 'Lady Maude, you would have an easier life if you did not use your tongue to cut so sharply. And if you did not go out of your way to annoy Lady Johanna so much. You could at least try to be more like a proper lady.'

Maude sat up. 'You know that nothing really pleases her. Nothing in Bunratty. She just doesn't want to be here; she wants to be back in England, she hates the Irish and she hates Thomond.'

'You may have the right of it, child. She is not a happy woman, but she had no choice. She was wed to Sir Richard when she was hardly older than you, and brought here to deal with all the troubles we have had in the last few years: Sir Richard out fighting the Irish, and her never knowing where he was or when he would come back; then the great battle here at the castle – oh, it must be seven summers since. And then the town being burnt by the Irish, and then the bad years, with freezing winters and summers where the rain never stopped. No wonder she wants to be with her own people. And she fears for the child. Especially as …'

'Especially as what?'

Margaret compressed her lips. 'I should not tell you, but you will no doubt hear it soon anyway. She will have another child in the autumn, another heir to Bunratty.'

'Oh Christ's blood!' said Maude. 'And no doubt I will be dragged in to look after it. That's all we need here, another screamer.'

Matthieu gave a small laugh. 'My sister is not a lover of babies,' he said.

'So I see,' said Margaret. 'Well, let's hope the child still has a father when it's born, for the way things are at the moment it seems likely he won't.'

'Is Sir Richard going off to the wars again, then?'

'Very soon, they say. But not until after they hunt the Silver Stag. You heard that it has been seen in the forest? The hunt is planned for two days' time; they say many lords will come to Bunratty to be part of it. We're going to be very busy and we only have two days to prepare. Knowing Sir Richard, he will use the opportunity to talk to them of campaigning as well as hunting.'

Maude realised that they too would only have two days to prepare to save the stag. 'Is Prior Outlaw coming?' Maude's voice was eager, and Matthieu stopped his drawing to wait for Margaret's response.

But she said: 'That I know not, only that there will be many more mouths to feed. More work, and more trying to stretch what little food we do have. Now, I can't stop here talking to you, I must get back to the kitchens. That blue gown you ripped has been mended, so you must wear that tonight. I'll take the red one for cleaning and have it ready for when the visitors come.'

When Margaret left, Maude got up and began to wander around the room restlessly. She went to the window and looked out.

'The rain has cleared. Let's go upstairs and practise archery. We can get Tuan to come too.'

Matthieu sighed, but put down his slate. He didn't want to go out to practise, but he knew that once Maude had made up her mind she would not leave him alone until he agreed to do what she wanted. Sometimes Matthieu thought Maude should have been the boy; she would have made a better knight than she did a young lady. She was faster, braver and stronger than he was and she enjoyed doing all the things that knights had to learn to do. She knew how to ride well, how to handle a lance and sword, how to use a bow and arrow. All these things Matthieu hated, mainly because he was very bad at them. He was clumsy and he did not see things in the distance very well. By far his most hated lesson was the tourney, learning the techniques of how you could unseat your opponent from their horse and not get hurt yourself. When he practised this, Matthieu spent most of the time on his back on the ground, for when he missed the target, it would swing around and knock him off his horse. Then Matthieu would lie in the dust and watch Maude fly past him, and with the tip of her lance hit the dead centre of the quintain, making it look as if it were the easiest thing in the world to do. His father had never said anything to him about his lack of skill, but Matthieu had sometimes caught a look of disappointment in his eyes.

But his father had been proud of him in other ways. He had been pleased with the way Matthieu would get up out of the dirt and keep trying, again and again and again. And he had praised him for his talent at drawing, and the fine letters he wrote, far clearer than Maude's though she was two years older. His mother, from what he could remember of her, had sung and played the lute, and his father had loved Matthieu's skill in music because it reminded him of her. Matthieu was desperately out of practice with his lute play- ing, for here in Bunratty there were no lutes to practise on, no musicians and no artists. Few enough people who could even read, apart from the sleepy old priest who came to teach him Latin and who only let him draw religious pictures or illuminate letters from the scriptures. He worried that he would lose all the skills he had in this savage place. Maybe things would get better now that Tuan had arrived; perhaps Maude would let him get on with his own life. And perhaps now there would be less time for his training, because from what Margaret said it seemed likely that preparation for serious battle would begin. Thankfully, he was still considered too young to go to battle, even as a squire. Though he had once overheard Sir Richard talking about him to Fat John.

'He needs to be blooded, John, to get a taste for the kill, like a hound.'

Fat John's voice was scornful. 'He's so small and weakly and unskilled, he'd be more trouble than he's worth at the moment. I could not see him handling himself well against the Irish.'

'Then it is about time he learned to do so,' said Sir Richard gruffly. 'Perhaps it is a case that when he has to do it he will learn some skill. I hate to see him wince when he is called out to practise. God's guts, his sister has more fire in her. She'd take the eye of an Irish kerne out of his head as soon as look at him.'

Fat John laughed. It was not a nice laugh. 'True enough. She needs to learn that her place is in the kitchen or the hall and not annoying my men, begging them for lessons with the sword and bow.'

The thing was, Matthieu actually loved the *idea* of knighthood, of chivalry and courage and adventure. He loved the stories of King Arthur and his knights pursuing the Holy Grail and their defence of the weak and innocent, the idea of valour in the face of impossible odds. He loved the pictures the stories made in his head, of the grace of the archer bending the bow or the skill of the swordsman's dance. He just hated the reality of the training, his clumsiness, the pain, the humiliation of always failing. Entering the training ground felt, every single time, like entering hell.

Now Maude was tussling with him, dragging him out of the room. They only had a short time before they had to go to eat in the Great Hall.

And the children must find time too for something much more important – time to come up with a plan that would save the stag.

CHAPTER 7

THE GREAT HALL

hen Tuan entered the Great Hall that evening, it was already crowded and filled with noise. People were crushed onto the benches and it didn't look as if the hall could hold any more, but more men still pushed their way in through the doors, shouting loud greetings to their comrades. Most of them were soldiers, who made their living through battle, their faces showing every possible variation of scar and bruise. At least half a dozen of them had broken noses. They had all been called in from the outer reaches of De Clare's territories.

The noise and movement was making Tuan feel dizzy. Mixed with the smell of roasting meat was that of the wicks burning in fat, and, in the heat of the hall, the smells of all the people around him. At least he was far away from Fat John. He shook his head to clear it and tried to hear what Sir Richard was discussing with the Captain – no doubt their plan for the hunt, or was it battle talk? He was too far from Matthieu and Maude to speak to them, although he had been given the honour of being seated above the place where the huge silver salt-cellar, shaped like a stag, sat in the centre of the table. Only servants and soldiers sat below the salt. He noticed that Maude, further up the table, was listening intently. Maude would tell him later what was being said. Earlier that day, they had agreed that they would all try to gather as much information as they could about the planned hunt of the Silver Stag.

Maude was able to overhear most of the conversation at the head of the table. Sir Richard was saying: 'The capture of the stag will give our men, and those of our allies, courage for the battles ahead. It will lift everybody's spirits.'

'And if you do not catch it?' asked Lady Johanna.

Sir Richard gave her a sour look. 'That is not something we will consider, my lady. We will kill the stag just as we will defeat Turlough O'Brien.'

'Is that who we are fighting now?' said Lady Johanna, her voice still scornful. 'It is so hard to keep up with all the changes.'

'I have explained to you before – we support the Irish clans that acknowledge our lordship. But that can change. They often try to use our alliances in their own petty wars. But the fact that they spend so much time fighting one another helps us to keep them under control.'

Maude smiled. The Irish were not the only ones who battled with each other all the time. The Norman English also fought each other for control of the land and people. She had tried to follow the various alliances Sir Richard had been part of since she had come to Ireland, but had given up. But one thing was clear: most of his alliances with the Irish were made because these Irish were enemies of some of the other great Norman lords in Ireland. And the Irish knew this, and used this knowledge for their own ends in their own wars. She still thought Margaret's description was the best she had heard: 'No wonder they call these lands the Swordlands. The Irish fight the Irish and the English fight the English and they both fight each other. That's Thomond for ye.'

Now, Maude could not resist saying, 'But I thought it was part of the code of knighthood to be loyal to your alliances and keep your word?'

Sir Richard's frown deepened. He hated being

reminded of previous alliances.

'It's politics, child, you would not understand. Women and children can never understand such things.'

Cliar caught Maude making a face as he said this. The sight of her crossing her eyes was so comical that Cliar could not help giving a yelp of laughter, and she almost spilled the ale she was pouring into Fat John's cup. He growled and grabbed her arm, twisting the flesh to make his grasp even more painful.

'What, witch girl? Do you mean to drown me?' he said.

Sir Richard frowned and pricked Fat John's arm with the point of his knife, so the Captain dropped the arm he was twisting.

'Let the child get on with her work,' said Sir Richard. 'Now, about the hunt. Robert, we need to discuss tactics,' he called to his Marshal, who was seated further down the table. Maude and Matthieu began to listen intently and Cliar spent a long time wiping the table close to where the Marshal sat, even though it did not need to be cleaned at all. 'I want you to send men out tomorrow into the woods to find the stag's trails and start marking out the territory where it has been. I have sent messengers to the local lords to join us here on Thursday evening and we will have the hunt on Mayday, the day after that. It will be a suitable day for the hunt. That will give you, my lady' – he nodded towards Lady Johanna – 'a chance to organise accommodation and food. Let us hope the weather will improve before then.'

'Are you inviting any of the Irish allies?' Lady Johanna's lip curled at the thought of entertaining Irish lords.

Sir Richard shook his head. 'No. Hunts are dangerous, and not just because the animals we hunt can attack us. I have heard stories of hunts that have gone terribly wrong ... it is far too easy for a stray arrow to hit a man. And between the confusion of the hunt and the darkness of the forest who can say it was anything but an accident? In any case, the Irish would refuse to hunt the Silver Stag – they hold it in some kind of superstitious veneration.'

'They say it is a magical beast,' said Robert the Marshal. 'And no other stag I have ever heard of has been silver.'

'Silver or gold, it will end up in the pot and its antlers will be hung on the wall of this hall. I am Lord of Bunratty and that is my word.'

✳ ✳ ✳

The children were very busy in the two days before the hunt. Cliar spent a lot of time running down to the mill in the

village and each time she came back she carried a mysterious bundle. Maude and Tuan went to the forest each day
and returned with equally mysterious and rather smelly
bundles which they hid in Tuan's tiny chamber. Tuan had
objected strongly to using his room as a store, but Maude
pointed out that the smell of pig and hen would disguise any
other bad smell that might cause suspicion among the servants of the castle. Matthieu made friends with Robert the
Marshal, who was also Master of the Hounds, displaying a
totally new interest in hound lore and hunting, and keeping
a sharp eye on where Robert kept the store of raw offal
which he fed to the hounds every night.

Cliar finally told the others about the ghostly inhabitants
of the castle who might be able to help them with their plan
to save the stag. Her secret had been found out at one of
their many meetings. Tuan and Cliar had joined Maude and
Matthieu in their room and Maude had been talking. Suddenly, she stopped and said to Cliar: 'What is it, Cliar? Why
do you sometimes look as if you're listening to someone
who isn't there?'

Cliar said nothing for a moment. Should she tell them
what she kept from everyone, even Margaret? Like everyone else in the castle, they obviously could not see or hear

anything out of the ordinary.

'It's the ghosts,' she said finally. 'I'm the only one in the castle that can see them. They are the people who lived here before us. People have been settled here for a long, long time – they say that the Danes had a camp here, long before the Normans sailed up the river, and before them the Irish kings held court here.'

Matthieu interrupted: 'Who were the Danes?'

'They were pirates and robbers who attacked the monasteries and stole their gold and killed the monks. It was Brian Boru, the ancestor of the O'Briens of Thomond, who drove them out of Ireland.'

When Cliar paused, Tuan added, unable to keep a smile off his face, 'They say the Danes, the sea pirates, are the ancestors of the Normans ...'

Cliar, noticing that Maude was about to say something, continued quickly: 'Everything that happened here has left a mark – the battles and the murders and the betrayals, and the good times too. The feasts and the laughter and the children who played here. They are all around us, all the time, filling the air. The man who built the original castle, down nearer the village, Sir Robert De Muscegros, he's quite fat and jolly most of the time. Some of the ghosts don't talk at all – Sir Thomas, Sir Richard's father, the first of the De Clares to come here, just floats around and looks disapproving. Lady Maude, Sir Richard's mother, is nice, though very sad. A lot of them are sad. Brian Rua, the Irish chief Sir Thomas killed, is probably the most unhappy of all. He does a lot of chain-clanking and lamenting.'

'I think I might have heard him one night,' said Matthieu excitedly. 'But is everyone who lived in Bunratty here?'

Cliar shook her head. 'Not everyone. I think only the ones who have something bothering them. The unfinished business keeps them here. They do no harm, though. Lots of them are my friends.'

'Is there a boy as well, a small boy with red hair?' Matthieu was remembering a particular face that would sometimes come at dusk, in the shadows of his room – though mostly, as he was falling into sleep, he thought he saw his father, and would talk to him about all the things that worried him. But sometimes he saw other faces; children in strange clothes, who smiled at him shyly.

Cliar nodded and began to speak, but Maude interrupted. She was impatient to get back to planning the stag's rescue.

'Matthieu, you know all that stuff you see is probably

your imagination, or something you have eaten,' she scoffed.

Cliar said, 'Anyway, I'd better go back to the kitchens. The White Ferret is on the warpath today.'

Maude giggled. 'Is that what you call Lady Johanna?'

Cliar laughed. 'That's what everyone in the kitchens calls her.'

'What is going on here?' A voice came from the doorway. Lady Johanna was there, looking none too pleased to see any of them.

She really did look like a white ferret, thought Tuan. He had only seen a ferret once; the Normans had introduced them to hunt rabbits. Lady Johanna, with her nose twitching and her small, pale eyes, slightly red-rimmed, and her white-blond hair, looked as if she would snap a rabbit in two as soon as look at it.

'Get back to the kitchens, girl,' she said to Cliar. 'And take the hostage back to his room. There is much to be done, for we need to prepare for the visitors that will be coming here for the hunt.'

✳ ✳ ✳

Two days later the castle was full to the brim and Lady Johanna was delighted to see the visitors; she loved to show off her English clothes and English ways. Unfortunately, her delight did not make her easier to live with, as she wanted everything to be even more perfect than usual. Margaret grumbled that she was sick and tired of running up and down to the solar for a new set of orders.

'How can I get anything done with me spending my time listening to her complain about everything? And mark my words,' she shook her finger at Cliar, 'no good will come of this hunt. Feasting on May Eve when the fairies are out and about and then going off to hunt a magical creature on Mayday morning. It's crazy. Sir Richard should be making sure the charms are put in place to protect his horses and cattle from harm, not making merry and going into the Good People's own territory on their special day.'

※ ※ ※

But make merry they did, in the Great Hall the night before Mayday. Because of the visitors, Maude and Matthieu were sent down the table to sit beside Tuan, and a group of musicians played (very badly in Matthieu's estimation) some tunes on recorder and harp. Cliar came and stood behind the other children as they began to eat. 'Remember what I told you about the bread,' she whispered. 'Be careful not to eat any.'

Tuan started guiltily. He had been so transfixed by the strange music that he had already nibbled a piece of his trencher. Within a few minutes, he began to feel very strange. Either there was no air coming into the hall or he was going to faint. But he had never fainted in his life. He looked around him. The hall was full of smoke, and the figures moved through it, in a fog so dense he could hardly recognise them. The talk around him was a buzz of bees, a flock of starlings in winter, a tribe of gannets exchanging news on their cliffside homes along the seacoast. And now the flames were dancing in the darkness, like the priests' stories of hell. And where Sir Richard and the Lady Johanna had been sitting, there was a hawk and a stoat. Fat John, to their right, had his place taken by a boar with huge tusks and bristles all over his face. Tuan looked down at his own hands, and was somehow not surprised to see that they were covered in fur, and instead of nails there were claws at the end of his fingers. Of course: Cú na Mara, the sea-dog or otter. His tribe's totem animal. What else could he have become?

Someone, something, touched him on the arm, and he jumped. Even so close, he could hardly make out the features of the face that was peering down at him through the smoke. Surely that was a pony – a pony with a kindly expression, but nonetheless a pony? He shook his head and the room swirled around. He felt very sick.

'Tuan, what's wrong? Are you not well?' The voice came from the rough-haired little pony by his side. It was Cliar. He shook his head and tried to get up. Staggering out of the hall, a hoof under one arm and a claw (was that young lioness Maude?) under the other, he was led out under the stars. The brightness outside and the cold air rushing into his lungs made him gasp and he promptly fell onto his knees, vomiting.

'Good, get it out of your stomach. It's the rye bread,' said the pony. 'You must have eaten some. You should have remembered what I said!'

Cliar had been busy the day before. Margaret had once told her to be careful of using rye flour, for if the weather was wet, a form of fungus called ergot could develop in it. Cliar had gone to the mill and had taken some of just such flour, which had been thrown out by the miller. She had mixed it into the bread for the feast. It would not kill anyone, but it would have the effect of making everyone who ate it see strange things and give them very bad head-aches and sick stomachs. It would ensure that no-one would be in the best of form for the hunt the next day.

Cliar and Maude walked Tuan around and held him steady while he cleared his stomach, and by the time the feast was over, the sickness had passed and in Tuan's eyes they had all taken human form again.

Then the children prepared to carry out their other plans to sabotage the hunt, plans that would keep them busy most of the night of that moonlit May Eve.

CHAPTER 8

THE STAG HUNT

ext morning, there was a huge breakfast set for the hunters in the Great Hall. Cliar was run ragged, bringing in dish after dish. She noticed that much of the food was sent back, uneaten. Many of the hunters looked as if they would rather be in bed than heading out for a day in the forest.

She had seen hunts at Bunratty before, but never one with so many people and never one that seemed so important to Sir Richard. He had sent Robert the Marshal out again and again to look for signs of the stag, and then the hunt had been planned like a military campaign. They now knew that the stag was in the eastern part of the wood, and the plan was to move it westwards, to the clearing known as Shepherd's Dell, where the archers and the mastiffs would be waiting to take it down. Of course, as in any campaign, things could change in the course of the hunt. That was half the adventure of it, the excitement of the chase.

Out in the bailey, the noise of the hounds was unbelievable. Gile became wildly excited with the racket. He strained on the cord that Maude had attached him to, first barking madly and then going into a sort of frenzied whimper of excitement. It was a beautiful morning, and in the distance the forest, with its fresh green leaves, looked like a magical place – or, thought Matthieu, an illustration in one of the Books of Hours he loved to look at. The hunters wore bright colours and even the most staid of the horses pranced around, pulsing with excitement.

'It looks so beautiful,' said Cliar. 'Such a pity it's all to kill something as wonderful as the stag.'

'Come on, Cliar, I've got a horse for you.' Maude's pale cheeks were rosy and her eyes were like stars.

'How did you manage that?' Cliar was astonished. The only servants usually allowed to go on a great hunt like this were the huntsmen, who led the dogs when they were not in pursuit of the stag, and the beaters, whose job it was to beat down the ferns and brambles of the forest, frightening the quarry so that it would run from its cover.

'I have organised it all. Tuan has permission to come with us too.'

'What about Margaret? Won't she want me here to help with the preparations for tonight when everyone is back?'

'No, I've talked to her, and she says she has lots of extra help from the village and that you have been looking pale and a day out in the woods will do you good. Look, she even gave us some food in case we lose the hunt and decide just to have a picnic in the forest. And Robert has said you can ride Shelly – she's so stubborn and slow nobody else wants to take her, but he says you have a way with horses.'

Cliar looked at Maude with admiration. She had thought of everything. Standing beside her, Matthieu was grinning. Most of the time it was a pain to have a sister who liked to organise things so much for everyone, but sometimes it was very, very useful.

Lady Johanna rode by on a beautiful white palfrey. She was dressed in a magnificent purple dress with gold edgings and a scarlet and gold cloak. Her headdress was a tall red steeple, hung with a fine golden veil. Her horse's bridle was hung with tiny golden bells. It was a pity, as Maude said, that she was wearing a face that would turn the milk sour, her thin mouth turned downwards and her eyes screwed up into a frown. She gave a cold glance at the children, but was too concerned with keeping her long, trailing outfit out of the mud to pay much attention to them.

'I wonder how far she'll get in that dress?' said Maude.

'Oh, she'll just go out as far as the edge of the wood,' said Cliar, 'and then she'll come back. She just likes to show off her clothes to as many people as possible. She doesn't like to get dirty.'

Maude snorted.

Tuan came riding up on Bellvoir, a young bay, smiling. 'Isn't it great that we all get to go along with the hunt?'

Cliar smiled back at him. 'Yes, it will make everything easier, hopefully.' Her stomach was full of butterflies. Their plan had to work …

The Marshal was explaining to Matthieu the progress of the hunt. In larger hunts they used separate packs of different kinds of dogs for tracking the game. But the Bunratty pack consisted of a mix of hounds of various breeds, mainly running-hounds and greyhounds. Sir Richard's great mastiff, Grandcour, led the pack. Cliar's heart almost stopped when she saw its great slobbering jaws and realised that those same cruel teeth would soon sink into the stag if the hunt was a success. She had a vivid image of the Silver Stag fallen, it's flesh torn and bloodied by the evil points of the arrows and the steel heads of the lances and spears. She crossed her fingers. They would not let that happen. They *could* not let that happen.

Robert was saying: 'Lady Johanna, now, she would know about the great hunts, even the royal hunts in England. They are something to see, I'm sure, but even here we do not put on too bad a show. That's a fine horse she has, Belami; brought all the way from France it was. And Sir Richard's horse, Beauvallet, is a beauty – as fine an example of a destrier as you are likely to see; though some say they are too heavy a breed for hunting. You children must stay well at the back, so as not to interfere with what is going on. You, young Mathieu, you must watch carefully so that later you will know what to do when you are a part of it, when you are Sir Matthieu. You must watch what happens when the stag is brought down by the dogs and the archers. It is Sir Richard's right to give it the *coup de grace*, the blow of the sword that ends its life. And you will see how we keep the dogs off the quarry so as not to ruin the meat. Cutting the meat is a skilled job and must be done properly. Then, Matthieu, we can blood you with the stag's blood. After that we let the dogs have their share.'

The Marshal looked around and sighed. 'I've never seen such a quiet lot of hunters, though. They must have spent too long at the wine. I don't feel too great myself, but I won't let that stop me making this hunt a day to remember. You look dreadfully pale too, boy. But the ride will soon bring colour to your cheeks'

Matthieu was pale because he was afraid he was going to be sick. Being blooded was a tradition at one's first hunt – after the kill, the blood of the dead animal was smeared over your face.

Maude went over and gave his shoulder a little shake. 'Don't worry,' she said. 'We won't let any of it happen.'

She sounded more confident than she felt. She felt responsible for how things went, for their plan that had been largely of her making, though Tuan had also added suggestions and Cliar had come up with the idea to add ergot to the bread.

✳ ✳ ✳

The Marshal rode over to Sir Richard and spoke to him. Sir Richard nodded. The hunt was called to order with the horn, and set out towards the forest. When they reached the trees at its edge, Lady Johanna and her ladies turned back and the rest of the hunt continued into the darkness of the forest.

The baying hounds, the jingling harnesses and the calls of the huntsmen to one another drowned out the birdsong that usually filled the wood.

The hunt had entered the eastern edge of the wood, and green branches folded over the riders' heads. Yellow gorse and drifts of bluebells grew in the small patches between the trees. At first they followed a path, but it became narrower and more overgrown as they travelled on, and eventually petered out altogether. Maude shivered as she spotted a cluster of feathers under her horse's hooves; a fox or a bird of prey had been busy hunting the night before. She did not like the forest. She preferred open spaces where, she told herself, you could see your enemy approaching from the distance. She would never admit it to anyone, but the forest scared her. Cliar looked at Maude's pale face and wondered at her nervousness. She felt sheltered in the forest, as if the trees were placing their branchy arms around her, enfolding her as a mother might her child. She led the group of children as they trailed behind the hunters, the dogs leading the chase, now baying in full voice.

There was a flash of something bright between the trees and the dogs went mad with excitement, picking up speed and tearing through the undergrowth so that the hunters could barely keep up with them. Another flash of silver, and then it was impossible to watch, for the horses were crashing through the bushy undergrowth of brambles and brushwood and new ferns, and bringing the hunters further and further into the heart of the wood.

At the back of the hunt, the children exchanged anxious glances. They would soon know if any of their efforts had been successful.

At first it seemed that their plan had not worked at all. The hounds pursued a single course under the trees, baying loudly, the huntsman's horn calling them on.

But then things began to go wrong. One of the hounds stopped and lifted her head. She sniffed the air, paw raised, as if puzzled by something. Then she suddenly took off into the undergrowth to the left of her path, away from her companions. Some of the other dogs ran after her, five or six of them following a trail away from the main hunt. The main body of the pack kept running forward, along with Sir Richard and the Marshal, but several huntsmen exchanged glances and made after the straying hounds, so that the hunt was split. The children looked at each other and smiled. Within a few minutes the same thing had happened again; some more of the hounds took off at a tangent, and several hunters followed them.

'It's working perfectly,' said Maude.

There was the call of a horn far in the distance, and the main body of the hunt, with Sir Richard at its head, drew to a halt.

'It's the sighting call,' said Sir Richard. 'Let's go east.'

'But the tracks are going this way,' said the Robert, his forehead wrinkled in puzzlement.

The horn called again.

'Quickly, now.' Sir Richard spurred his horse and led the way eastwards.

The children watched.

'That store of honey I gave young Bat, the miller's son, was well worth it,' said Cliar with satisfaction.

'Just be sure he gets the hunting horn back to us safely,' said Maude. 'It was my father's.'

But then there was another call, a thin, eerie one, from the south.

'Did he get his friends to help out?' asked Matthieu, puzzled.

Cliar shook her head. The horn called again from the north.

'It's the ghosts,' she said. 'They said they would help us;

it's a ghost horn, leading the hunters astray... nobody will know which way to go!'

'I wonder where the stag actually is?' asked Matthieu.

That had been their worry all through the night, when they had carefully laid false trails of deer droppings and fresh meat all over the forest. The plan had been to throw the dogs into such confusion that the hunt would have to be abandoned. The after-effects of the ergot and the hunting horn calls from different directions would confuse the hunters further; one could only hope that by some piece of bad luck the hunt would not actually come upon the stag.

'It looks like the plan has worked. Let's go home,' said Matthieu, who was getting tired and who had had enough excitement for one day. His stomach had felt sick all morning, from worry that they might not succeed with their plan. 'We can't really do any more, can we?'

'Oh, don't be such a baby,' said Maude. 'We have to make sure that Sir Richard gives up the hunt. Anyway, this is a chance to spend the day away from the castle. No-one has any idea where we are and they won't care until everyone has returned home. If they even notice we're missing then. Let's have the food Margaret gave us.'

✳ ✳ ✳

Soon, not only had the hunt gone out of sight, but the children could not even hear the dogs or the horses.

'Let's follow the stream a little way and see where it brings us. If we hear the hunt we can always move away.' Tuan led the way through the hazel bushes that overhung the clear stream that wound its way along the forest floor. There was no noise now, apart from the rustle of their horses' hooves through the dry leaves that had fallen the previous winter. Over their heads the new spring leaves formed a bright green canopy, and through it the sky was an intense blue.

Within a few minutes thay had come to a clearing in the wood. In the centre was a pool of dark water that reflected the sky above. It was surrounded by young silver birch trees, and the trees too were reflected in the pool, the light moving as the branches swayed in the breeze. There was something about the place that made them all pull up their horses and dismount, then stand perfectly still. No-one said anything; they listened, but there was no sound apart from a cuckoo's call through the trees. Then it too went silent.

On the other side of the pool there was a rustle in the green branches. The sky through these branches seemed a deeper blue, a translucent colour that was almost violet, the colour of young bluebells. The heat buzzed with the intense stillness of midday. The horses remained as still as statues. Gile stood, one paw raised, as if he too had been turned to stone.

In the depths of the wood, something bright was moving. The brightness moved quietly out of the trees and faced them across the still pool. None of them could ever properly describe it afterwards, though it appeared in their dreams all through their lives. Matthieu spent many years trying to capture its beauty in paint. Green leaves behind, blue sky above, the dark pool – a silver shadow gleaming in the depths of the pool like moonlight on water. The Silver Stag raised its head and its great silver antlers branched out like bare, shining trees on either side of its proud and gentle forehead. Its eyes were dark and its glance towards the children held no fear. It was all grace, all dignity, but a dignity that was without arrogance. It was simply itself and did not need to be anything else.

None of them could speak. There was a feeling of absolute stillness – stillness and light. The horses stood with their heads bent, as if in homage. Even Gile remained totally motionless, watching, but not fearful, his ears upright and his eyes very bright.

The time they stood there could only have lasted a moment, for then came the noise of hounds in the distance and the call of the horn.

'They're coming,' said Cliar, her throat dry with panic. 'The hunt is coming this way.'

The stag still stood, motionless as a figure in a tapestry, its beautiful head raised, watching them. Waiting for them.

Tuan and Maude jumped onto their horses; afterwards, neither could remember who thought of it first.

'Quick, mount and ride,' called Tuan. 'We'll lead the hunt towards the Shannon, to the grasslands; if the stag crosses the water the hounds will lose its trail.'

At the same moment, Maude pointed to the river. 'Come, let's go that way.'

Strangely enough, none of them thought to question whether the stag would follow them.

Cliar nodded, and they all set off through the under-growth, crashing through ferns and pushing their horses to go as fast as they could. The horses sensed the urgency, and even old Shelly, famous for her laziness, broke into a gallop, or as much of a gallop as was possible in the dense undergrowth of the wood.

And the stag followed them.

But now as they raced onwards they could hear the sound of the hunt coming nearer. Closer and closer all the time. At the edge of the forest they broke into a full gallop. The stag ran by their side through the river fields.

Maude looked behind her and said breathlessly: 'They're coming closer. We have to go faster.'

Faster they went, Matthieu clutching onto his horse's mane for dear life. But they could feel the hunt gaining on them. Matthieu began to panic; he felt that he himself was now the quarry of the hunt. He could almost feel the hot breath of the hounds on his heels; he could almost feel their sharp teeth sinking into his flesh ... But he held on, and pushed his horse onwards. The stag had to be saved.

Tuan glanced back. The first hounds had come out from the edge of the wood with the horses close behind. We won't make it, he thought, we cannot make the river ...

But just as the hunt was about to close in, something very strange happened.

The dogs stopped dead. Their ears flattened. Their tails dropped between their legs. They began to whimper. Then the horses stopped dead too, and reared upwards, unseating some of their riders. They whinnied in fear and pranced around, as if terrified by something the huntsmen could not see. The cavalcade became a shambles of neighing horses and dogs that whined and growled and backed away, back into the edge of the wood, as if an invisible wall was pushing them away from the water's edge.

'It's the ghosts!' said Cliar. 'They're helping us again.'

Now the stag had reached the river bank. It stopped for a moment, as the children looked back to the hunt. The animals were refusing to come nearer, despite the shouts and curses and spurrings of Sir Richard and his companions, desperate to move them on towards the stag.

The great beast looked at the children for a moment, a moment only, and then leapt into the water and began to swim upstream. The four children stood silently, watching the silver figure of the stag move away and become one with the shimmering water.

※ ※ ※

Moments later the first dogs had arrived, howling at the river as if trying to make it give back their prey. The Marshal rode up to the children, his face like thunder.

'Didn't I tell you to keep to the back of the hunt?' he roared. 'You have driven the stag to the river. The bloody beast has escaped us – we'll never pick up the trail now.'

'We didn't drive the stag anywhere,' said Maude, her voice and face as haughty as she could make it.

Sir Richard rode up, red-faced. 'What? But didn't we just see you drive the stag here?'

'No, we did not,' said Maude again. 'We did not drive the stag anywhere.' It came with us, she thought. We didn't drive it. It's almost the truth.

'Then why the devil did it come this way?' Sir Richard sounded weary rather than angry. 'Well, we'll never get the dogs or the horses to swim across there. In any case, they seem possessed by spirits today; I have never seen such a fiasco from beginning to end.'

'Aye,' said Robert, who looked deeply perplexed and ashamed. 'A cursed hunt if ever I saw one. What the devil got into the horses and hounds at the edge of the wood? It minds me of the stories of the wild hunts they tell of in the south, in Knockainy – of spirit hounds coming to fetch a soul.' He shivered. 'I hope it is not one of ours,' he said.

'That is all Irish nonsense,' said Sir Richard. 'It must have been something they ate. You must look to your dog boys, Robert, and find out what has been going on. But, then, the horses were no better ... Well, the sport is over for the day, it seems. Come. Let's get back to the castle. The sky is dark –

that evil wind has brought rain with it as well as ill luck.'

It was true, and soon the rain poured down, making all the bright clothes wet and bedraggled.

When they got back to the castle, soaked and exhausted, there was a great bustle inside. Margaret saw the children enter and she almost dragged Cliar down from her horse.

'I need you in the kitchen, and look at the state of you. Get out of your wet clothes and then come straight down. Tonight we have to feed many mouths and on top of everything else, an unexpected guest has arrived.'

CHAPTER 9

Prior Roger Outlaw

It was Roger Outlaw, Prior of the Hospitallers, and half a dozen of the brothers with him.

'More work,' Margaret grumbled. 'As if we hadn't enough to do with all the hunters here.'

Tuan had vaguely heard of Prior Roger, but he whispered to Maude: 'Who is he? Who are the Hospitallers?'

'Haven't you heard of the Hospitallers?' said Maude, with a touch of her old, scornful tone.

Tuan dug deep in his memory. 'Maybe. They're English Normans, and they fight the Irish too, don't they?' he said.

'They are monks, well, sort of monks, but they're knights and soldiers as well,' said Maude. 'The order was founded to protect the pilgrims in Jerusalem. Now they have houses all over Europe – my father is fighting with them in Rhodes.

That's where their headquarters are. Prior Roger doesn't just fight the Irish, though. Actually he's friendly with lots of the Irish tribes. That's why he's often sent out to make peace with the Irish, to make treaties. And he has come to Thomond to get the English lords to sit down and talk to one another. He is the most famous man in Ireland for getting people to talk to one another, and he's a great soldier too. The Hospitallers are famous for their skill in battle and for their skill in politics. But they look after people who are sick and wounded too, and pilgrims.'

'It's little enough of looking after the sick and wounded Prior Outlaw does,' said Margaret, overhearing. 'And though they say the hospitality of Kilmainham is second to none, it isn't for pilgrims, but for the rich that it is provided. Prior Outlaw himself is a fine man, a clever man, who has the ear of the great and rich of the land, the ear of the king himself in England, it is said. And he's a good friend of Dame Anna. There are some say they're related.'

Cliar nodded. 'He has always been kind to me too,' she said.

'Well, Cliar, get into the kitchen now, I'll need your help with the sugar swans,' said Margaret. 'And the rest of you go and change those wet clothes instead of getting under my feet.' She turned to Maude and Matthieu. 'Her ladyship will want you two to be dressed in your best when you meet Prior Outlaw. I'll send Allison up to help you when she has finished in the kitchen.'

✳ ✳ ✳

When Tuan entered the Great Hall to take his place at the table, the first thing he did was look up to the top of the table where Sir Richard sat with his guest at his right hand. Outlaw was a broad-faced man, with large, piercing green eyes and a thick mane of greying red hair brushed back from his face. He had a scar on his right cheekbone. He was not at all like any monk Tuan had ever met. He did not even wear a monk's robe, but a white tunic with a red cross blazing across its front. At his side hung a large sword. As Tuan came in, Maude and Matthieu were being introduced to him, and he was smiling at them kindly. Yes, thought Tuan, he may be a kind man. But I don't think I would like to cross him.

'One of the cleverest men in Ireland,' Cliar whispered as she served Tuan his meat. 'They say he's as wily as a fox, that he can leave a room with everyone thinking they have got their own way, when they are all doing exactly what Prior Outlaw wants.'

He does look a bit like a fox, thought Tuan. It seemed that his hearing was as good as a wild animal's too, for Outlaw glanced down the table as if he had heard Cliar's whisper. Then he leaned his head towards Sir Richard and said something to him.

Sir Richard raised his voice. 'It seems that Prior Roger would like to meet our Irish guest. Come to the top of the table, boy.'

Tuan made his way up until he stood in front of Outlaw, and then he bowed.

'You are one of the Mac Conmaras, is that not so?' said Outlaw.

'Yes, of the Conall Mac Conmara branch. I am the son of Sorley Mac Conmara and Sive O'Dea,' said Tuan.

'A brave man, your father,' said Outlaw. 'I had dealings with him more than once. We will talk more later, perhaps.' He turned to Sir Richard. 'I understand that this boy and your two wards saw the escape of the Silver Stag today? It seems the legend that he will never be caught is a true one.'

Sir Richard grunted. 'We almost had him today. It was pure mischance that he made his way to the river. But, in any case, the hunt was a shambles from beginning to end –

sick heads and hounds that could not keep to the trail.' He sighed. 'No doubt there will be other days and other hunts. We will get him yet and his antlers will be hung on the walls of the castle, along with all the other game we have caught.'

'I have heard them say that fairy horns led the hunters astray too, and that all the misfortunes happened because the hunt was held on Mayday.' This was Lady Johanna, her voice spiteful.

Sir Richard turned his eyes upwards. 'Oh, no doubt that will be the story the Irish will tell. Along with their tales of banshees and fairy queens at Knockainy. Outlaw, you have spent time at the Hospitaller house at Knockainy, haven't you? Have you ever seen the fairy queen? What's this her name is – Áine?'

Outlaw smiled. 'I have seen many strange things in my life, Sir Richard. But I take it you have no time for tales of such things? Your mind must be on more immediate troubles. How goes it in this part of the country?'

Sir Richard sighed. 'As always: war and trouble. I have just today got news that the Mac Conmaras have been seen on the borders of our lands, rustling cattle. I will ride out tomorrow to see what the truth of it is. 'Tis true I have no time for fairy tales – women's fancies – with such things going on. Outlaw, tell me, what is the news from Dublin and the north?'

'Not good: war and famine. Lord, I would wish for a few years' peace where crops could grow and herds graze safely. Do you think we will see it in our lifetime?'

De Clare laughed. 'Perhaps in your quiet part of the country near Dublin. But not here. These are the sword-lands that can only be held by the sword. And, in truth, I would not live my life any other way. Time enough to rest when we are dead.'

Cliar jumped, nearly spilling the jug she was pouring from. In the moment's silence that followed what Sir Richard had said, she was nearly sure she heard Brian Rua, the ghost who had been killed in Bunratty, whisper in her ear: 'Which may be sooner than you think.'

CHAPTER 10

MIDNIGHT MEETING

It was deep night in Bunratty. Tuan was woken from sleep by Cliar shaking his shoulder. The moon shone through the window, a half-moon as bright as day.

'Come with me,' she said. 'Dame Anna and Prior Outlaw want to see us. Maude and Matthieu are already on the way to the tower.'

'What is it about? Why do they want to see *us*?'

Cliar shook her head. 'I don't know. I only know we all have to go there. Perhaps she wants to ask us about the stag.'

They made their way across the bailey and up the narrow staircase to the tower. The door swung open before them and they saw that the tower room was ablaze with light, moonlight and firelight mingling. Dame Anna and Outlaw were seated at the long table, and Maude and Matthieu were there with them. Matthieu was leaning his head on his folded arms, looking as sleepy as Tuan felt, but Maude's face was lit up with excitement.

'Welcome, children,' said Dame Anna. 'Welcome – and well done all of you. You saved the stag today and Tradree is in your debt. It seems that between the four of you, you can do great things. And great things may well be asked of you. For terrible times are coming upon us if Sir Richard does not listen to the advice of those who can see a little way into the future.'

'But first,' she turned to Maude and Matthieu, 'I know you have been wanting to ask Prior Roger something.'

Maude nodded and said, her words tripping over each other in her impatience: 'Prior Roger, have the Hospitallers heard any word from the east? Any word of my father who was fighting with them?'

Prior Roger shook his head. 'I am sorry that I cannot bring you any better news, little one. There is word that the battles in the east have not been going well, with many of our soldiers captured. But there has been no word of Sir Bertram. Have patience; there are brothers coming from Italy to Kilmainham soon, with letters for us from further east. Perhaps they will have more news.'

Maude nodded, swallowing the lump that seemed to have lodged in her throat. She would not cry. She could not show Matthieu that she too was frightened, that she too sometimes doubted if their father was still alive. He had to be, she thought, he had to come and save them from a life lived in this place, depending on the kindness of people who had no kindness in them.

Now, to her relief, Tuan changed the subject, asking Prior Roger, 'Excuse me, Prior, how do you and Dame Anna know one another?'

Outlaw laughed. 'I have known Dame Anna a long time, ever since I was a child at Knockainy, our house to the south of here. She could even be called my nurse. And I am related by marriage to her, distantly, through the Outlaws of Kilkenny. Your cousin, Dame Alice Kyteler, sends her greetings, Dame Anna.'

Dame Anna snorted. 'I will have no truck with my cousin Alice since she took to using her skills in the service of dark ways. She does not walk in the light anymore, and uses her powers to harm and hurt rather than help.'

There was a silence for a moment, as the children looked at Dame Anna expectantly. She sighed. 'Alice Kyteler is a woman who has special powers, some might say powers like mine – or like yours, Cliar. She has the power to heal, and she knows about herbs and potions, how they can be used to cure and how they can be used to harm. But she has used those powers badly. I foresee dark times ahead for her, if she does not change her ways. Outlaw, I do not know why you give her succour. Her ways are not yours, as you well know. And her ways may well end in disaster for those who keep her company.'

'That may be so, but she is still kin, and I have my loyalties. And I think, my Lady, that I am not one of the weak,' said Outlaw. They smiled at one another. 'But, look you, we need to speak of Sir Richard and what goes on here in the west rather than in the Pale.'

'I am afraid of what will happen if Sir Richard goes to fight the Irish,' said Dame Anna.

Prior Roger glanced at Tuan and said quietly: 'Are you sure it is good to be talking about such things in front of the Irish child? May he not want to see Sir Richard destroyed?'

As Outlaw's eyes met his, Tuan felt as if the Prior was trying to see into his very soul.

But Dame Anna smiled and said, 'Tuan, what say you?'

Tuan took a breath. 'I do not want to see Bunratty and its

people hurt. I have no love for Sir Richard, but he has treated me justly, and while I am his guest I would not betray him.'

'Well said, child,' said Prior Roger. 'Honestly and honourably put.' He smiled at Tuan.

'Very well,' he continued, 'I came here to Sir Richard to try to get him to come with me to parley with the clans of the south. It seems to me that we have the chance to be peacemakers between those who contest the Lordship of the O'Briens. But Sir Richard will not listen. He is afraid of looking weak, and he thinks to parley rather than to fight is a sign of weakness. I too can fight, but I would rather have this kingdom at peace. God knows, we have seen enough battles these past few years.'

Dame Anna nodded. 'There, I am with you. But perhaps I can see things more clearly if I look to the future.'

'Then perhaps you can warn him,' said Prior Roger. 'Maybe he will listen to you.'

'That is unlikely,' said Dame Anna. 'But already I have seen terrible things if Sir Richard goes to war. I have seen red blood flowing and the white towers of Bunratty destroyed in red flames.' She stood up and stared straight ahead as if she was in a trance. 'Red and white and black shall be Bunratty. I saw weeping and cursing and ships on the Shannon fleeing away from this place. Tell Sir Richard this. Warn him, Outlaw.'

The children stared, shocked.

Outlaw sighed. 'I will try, but his mood at the moment is impossible. You must talk to him, Dame Anna, for he listens to no-one but the Lady Johanna at the moment, and she loves me not at all – she sees me as an upstart, because my family is not as noble as hers. She does not even like my name, though it is many generations since my family acquired it! I myself will go first to the south to see what is happening at Knockainy.'

Tuan tried to block his ears. He didn't want to hear Outlaw's plan. He didn't want to help Sir Richard. Yet, if Sir Richard was defeated, the lives of Tuan's friends would be at risk. It had been so simple before he came to Bunratty: the foreigners – Norman and English – were the bad ones and the Irish the good ones. Now, it was different because of Maude and Matthieu and Cliar, and even people like Margaret, just ordinary people trying to get on with their lives. It was all very confusing.

But now Prior Outlaw was talking to him directly.

'Tuan, I will meet with your father and his clan. I have

had dealings with them these past months, and we trust each other. If you ever need to get back to your people, you must come to me. Do not try to go east through the woods alone. That part of the country is crawling with soldiers, and worse. I know ways that you can go to get home safely, if you are under my protection. Will you promise me that?'

Tuan nodded, a little reluctantly. He knew he would never leave Bunratty unless he was fetched by his people. It was a point of honour.

'Good,' said Outlaw. 'And as you are the only one here who knows about river craft and has travelled alone in the countryside of Thomond, you must be the one to listen to my directions. If you, any of you, need to come to me for help, you must seek me in Knockainy. It too is a journey that holds dangers, and do not undertake it unless you have no other choice. The Priory is four or five days' travel, through pastureland and forest. There are wild parts of the woods that are not safe, and you must go carefully. You must find the Maigue River and follow it. The first river branching off that is the Camog; pass that by, and go on until you come to where the Morningstar branches off. Follow this until you can see the hills of Lough Gur to the north. After that you must head east, by land, and soon you will see Knockainy, Áine's Hill, which is no more than four miles to the west of Hospital. That's where we knights live.'

Tuan hoped that somebody else was listening to the directions Outlaw was giving them, for what reason would he ever have to go to Knockainy?

'Excuse me, Prior,' said Maude. 'But why is Sir Richard fighting Turlough O'Brien now? It's so hard to keep up with what's happening ...'

'That is because the alliances change all the time. Sir Richard and his father, Sir Thomas, are alike in that. You know the story of Sir Thomas? How he hanged a visiting Irish prince, his comrade in the wars, from the walls of Bunratty?'

'That was Brian Rua,' said Cliar. 'No wonder he spends his time lamenting.'

Outlaw looked at her, then continued. 'What you have to remember is that the wars in Thomond are not just among the English and the Irish, but between different factions within the English and Irish people themselves. And loyalties can change overnight; for example, Sir Richard has always been an enemy of the De Burghs, but now Sir Richard wants to make an alliance with them so he can take on

Murtagh O'Brien, who is the greatest threat to the English lords.' He sighed, realising that he had succeeded in doing nothing but totally confusing the children, with the possible exception of Maude, who was listening intently.

'All you really need to know is that Sir Richard is never still and that he loves battle. He has been making wars from the time he was a child when he saw his father killed when Turlough O'Brien besieged Bunratty. What you do need to understand is that you must keep each other safe, as you saved the Silver Stag today. If the four of you keep together you will be able to do great things. This is why Dame Anna and I called you here tonight. But now I must leave, for the dawn is coming. Come down with me to the stables to see me off.'

'Yes,' said Dame Anna. 'All of you go, but Cliar, stay here. I have need of you, for I feel that we may require a store of medicines before this day is over.'

In the stables, Tuan petted Outlaw's beautiful horse as the Prior spoke urgently to Sir Richard, who had come to see his guest off. But the Lord of Bunratty did not even bother to answer the Prior, nor did he wait to watch Outlaw leave. Instead he turned away suddenly and made his way towards the north west tower, a frown on his face.

Prior Roger shrugged as he watched him go, then turned to Tuan and smiled.

'He's a wonderful beast, my Astrea, is he not?' said Prior Roger. 'He is of the Irish Hobby breed, horses so light and quick they are fit gifts for a king. If you come to see the Hospitaller house you will see many such. And you are welcome in any Hospitaller house, all of you,' he said. 'Dublin or Knockainy or wherever you should wish to come. May God preserve you all from harm in the times that are coming upon us.'

And then he was gone, with his servants riding around him. They watched him go, a tall figure on his great white horse, dressed in full armour to protect him on the road ahead.

CHAPTER 11

Dame Anna Foretells the Future

eft in the tower with Dame Anna, Cliar worked hard and said nothing. Usually she enjoyed being with Dame Anna, for as they worked the woman would explain the uses and properties of the various herbs they put into the potions they made. This morning, however, Dame Anna was silent and serious, and worked very quickly, not speaking a word other than brief commands to Cliar.

There was a knock at the door, and with hardly a pause, Sir Richard entered the tower room. He was alone, and his face was red – Cliar could not be sure if it was from anger or from the exertion of climbing the stairs.

Dame Anna looked at him, her eyebrows raised.

'And to what to I owe the'– she paused, as if considering what word to use 'pleasure of a visit from your Lordship?' she asked.

Sir Richard grunted. 'I take it I can visit any part of my own castle should I feel the desire? No particular reason.'

Dame Anna said nothing, just stood there, a bowl in her hands and her eyebrows still raised.

'Very well then, woman,' said Sir Richard. 'I want you to scry for me.' He noticed Cliar. 'And get that girl out of the room. This is serious business and we want no reports of what happens filtering down to the kitchens.'

'This girl will tell no-one in the kitchens what happens in this chamber, and I will need her to assist me. I am not as young as I used to be, Sir Richard.'

Sir Richard snorted. 'You look no different than you did years ago when this castle was built and you first came here. Indeed, I think you were never young.'

'Oh indeed I was, and indeed I am different now,' said Dame Anna. 'But let the girl stay. She is learning my craft. When I am no longer here you will need someone else to look to the future for you. If you outlast me, that is.'

'Very well, then, but let us get on with it. I have much to do.'

'First you must relax. Cliar, fetch his lordship a cup of the rosemary tisane we made last week. And sit yourself down, Sir Richard, while I prepare the scrying bowl.'

Dame Anna went about the preparations Cliar had seen many times before: instructing her to close the shutters so that the room was darkened except for the fire in its centre; laying herbs on the flames so that the room was filled with heavy, strange-smelling smoke; pouring the water from jug to basin and setting it in front of the fire so that the flames were reflected in it.

When Sir Richard had drunk the mixture Cliar had given him, and finally stopped twitching, he sat heavily slumped on the bench, his eyes hazy. His voice, when he spoke, had slowed down from his usual quick, barbed tones.

'What is it you wish to know?' asked Dame Anna.

'The outcome of the wars with the O'Briens.'

'And which clan of the O'Briens would that be, now? I have heard you have changed allegiance again. Do you ever keep your word?'

Now it was Cliar's turn to hold her breath. Anyone saying such a thing to Sir Richard under normal circumstances was risking their freedom, if not their life. But his lordship, under the influence of the potion and the scented flames, merely shook his head and smiled rather foolishly.

'Not unless I have to,' he muttered. 'Or it suits me. Now, tell me what you see of the fighting; how goes it to the north?'

There was a silence while Dame Anna stood gazing into the flame-filled water. Cliar watched too, fascinated by the way the fire was reflected in the silver bowl. As she watched she felt as if she too were seeing something in the water. Figures moved, faces came and went. Then she was no longer looking into the bowl; instead, the bowl had become a world she had entered. There were men in Irish dress that she did not recognise, meeting, talking together, clasping hands as if in agreement. She saw Sir Richard riding out on a bright morning, his army behind him, heading north towards the stony desert lands of the Burren. They rode for a long time through the great rock-covered landscape, where no grass grew, where no trees sheltered the rider from the wind coming in from the vast ocean, where there was no place to hide from an enemy.

She cried out. Now they were back in grasslands, and there was a grey stone church and a huddle of houses, and a river and some trees. But Sir Richard had been wounded. He was covered in blood and staggering towards the river.

He fell down face forwards into the water. In the background there were Irish soldiers, laughing in triumph. Someone came up behind him; she saw a raised axe and then found that she was being shaken by Sir Richard, who was cursing her.

'Why the devil did you call out like that and bring Dame Anna out of her trance? Curse you, child! And you' – he let Cliar drop and turned to Dame Anna – 'did you get a chance to see anything?'

'Aye, I saw what the child saw and what her made call out. I saw disaster for your troops and for yourself if you attack Dysert O'Dea.'

Sir Richard's face went white. 'How did you know that that was my plan? Did one of your accursed birds bring you news?'

'I saw the abbey and the land around. I saw the river and I saw the plain. Forget Dysert O'Dea, it will only bring ruin and death upon you, Sir Richard. Think of your lady wife and your child and the safety of those who are in the castle. Try to make peace with the Irish, for it is time for these wars to end. Have you and your family not broken enough vows and seen enough men and women die?'

Sir Richard sprang towards Dame Anna and for a

moment Cliar thought he was going to take her by the
throat. But instead he swept the basin aside and the water
spilled onto the floor, flowing towards the fire. Then he
turned and strode angrily from the room, slamming the
door so hard behind him that the frame shuddered. Cliar
looked at Dame Anna, who did not seem in the least bit dis-
composed.

'Run, child, and get a cloth to wipe up the water,' she
instructed.

Cliar nodded wordlessly, aware that there was no point in
asking Dame Anna questions when she decided she did not
want to say anything. When she came back to mop up the
spilt water, she noticed that, while it hissed and spat at the
edge of the fire, it showed no sign of dousing it.

She looked at Dame Anna and the lady looked back at
her, smiling slightly.

'It would take more than a fit of temper from Sir Richard
to douse those flames,' she said. 'I told him what I saw and I
can do no more if he refuses to listen.' She sighed. 'There
may be more flames in Bunratty than he has bargained for.'

'But there is something else that concerns me,' she continued. 'I saw something else in the flames. Sir Richard
plans to send a messenger within the next few days to tell

Outlaw to meet him at Dysert. This must not happen, Cliar. Outlaw, at least, will listen to me. I must get a message to him to tell him not to go.'

'Will you send him one of your pigeons?' asked Cliar.

Dame Anna smiled. 'I may ... But even that is a risk. We cannot catch up with him on the road, for Outlaw rides exceedingly fast. Go now, child, Margaret will be waiting for you to help her in the kitchens. But first take this.' She went to one of the shelves and unflasked a vial, measuring some drops carefully into a cup. 'Drink this. You must have a clear head, and you will be feeling strange after coming out of the trance.'

Cliar nodded. She did feel sick, and her head felt dizzy and throbbing. But even after she took the drink and her head cleared, she could not get the picture of Sir Richard out of her mind: he was falling, bloody and bent and cursing his fate.

CHAPTER 12

The Cattle Raiders

And Sir Richard prepared to go to war. The lords and ladies who had gathered for the hunt all left during the morning, subdued and silent. Originally, the plan had been to have a feast that night, with musicians and dancing in the Great Hall. Lady Johanna looked on furiously as her guests made their apologies and called for their horses from the stables.

'Well, we shall have the dancing in any case. It is all organised. And you, Richard, be sure that you are back for it.'

Her husband shrugged. 'My first duty is to ensure the safety of the lands around the castle. There have been rumours of cattle raids in the valleys to the east. I am going to ride out to see if they are true. I will bring Fat John and some of the guards with me – we can get rid of one menace, at least.'

He noticed Matthieu, who was trying to make himself as invisible as possible against the background of a tapestry.

He beckoned the boy over. 'Matthieu! You will come along too. It will be good experience for you. You need to see some real battles to prepare for your future as a knight.'

Matthieu swallowed and made his way to the stables.

Cliar went to see him off. 'Don't worry too much,' she said, with a confidence she did not feel. 'I'm sure you'll be fine. But where's Maude?'

Matthieu made a face. 'She's with Lady Johanna. She would love to be heading out instead of me!'

As the soldiers rode away, Cliar thought that poor Matthieu looked a miserable figure, hunched over his saddle. She looked up towards the window of the north west tower. She could just make out the long white hair and black gown of Dame Anna, who seemed to be watching as the patrol rode eastwards. But when she looked again, the figure was gone.

Maude, meanwhile, was arguing with Lady Johanna.

'What about me?' said Maude. 'Why couldn't I go with the patrol?'

'Because you are a young lady!' said Lady Johanna.
'You may help me organise things for the feast!'

Maude said angrily: 'I don't want to organise things for
the stupid feast! I want to ride out and see the battle!'

Lady Johanna grabbed Maude's shoulder and pulled her
upstairs to her bedroom. She pushed the girl onto her knees
at the *prie-dieu* and told her brusquely. 'Pray to Saint
Agnes, the patron of young girls, and at least try to follow
her in the ways of obedience.'

Maude knelt with her hands over her face, but she did not
pray to St Agnes. Most female saints were, in her view, a
waste of space. They were obedient and patient and did
nothing interesting. It was all very well being long-
suffering, but it didn't get you anywhere. She preferred the
warrior saints like St George and the hunters like Julian and
Matthieu, but on this occasion she did not pray to them
either. Instead she thought hard.

As soon as Lady Johanna had left, she went to the chest
where Matthieu's clothes were kept and began searching
through them ... She had seen the look on her brother's face
when Sir Richard had ordered him to go. The boy had been
terrified. She had to go with him; she had promised her
father to look after her younger brother. And, anyway,

Matthieu was not going to be the only one to have an adventure. She hoped that the rumours of cattle-rustling were true. She didn't want life in the castle to get boring again.

✳ ✳ ✳

Matthieu, riding behind Fat John and his lookalike son, whom he and Maude had privately named Even Fatter Godric, fervently hoped the opposite. Godric kept shouting at Matthieu to sit up in the saddle, occasionally poking him in the side with his sword to try to make him sit straighter. Godric was a worthy son of his father. He spent his time killing things and eating them. You could generally tell what he had eaten for dinner from the remains on his clothes and his moustache. He also smelt even worse than his father; his nickname in the kitchen was Stinker Two. And yet, despite his unpleasant appearance, he was incredibly vain. He did not seem to realise that the space that cleared around him as he made his way through the castle was not because people were in awe of him, but because nobody liked to be near him. Maude had seen him once, peering in a pewter plate to burst a pustule on his face. 'If I had a face like his,' she had said to Matthieu, 'I would avoid anything that gave a reflection for fear of catching sight of myself!'

The fact that it was a lovely day and that the lands they

were travelling through were bright with cowslips and haw-thorn didn't help Matthieu's mood at all. Normally, he would have enjoyed seeing all this beauty around him. But today all he could think of was the possibility of battle. They were travelling eastwards, towards the forest and uplands where the Mac Conmaras, Tuan's people, lived. Far too soon for Matthieu's liking, they had reached the hill that marked the boundary of Sir Richard's lands. A green field, cropped short by sheep and cows, stretched up towards a scatter of large, grey rocks at the top of the hill. There were some cattle grazing there, looking peaceful and content. The slope was covered in daisies and a small scattering of golden gorse bushes, bent almost double from the western wind. But it was also marked with the hooves of horses.

'The Irish have been here – look, we can follow their trail now,' said Sir Richard. 'There is a ravine on the eastern side of the hill, it falls steeply down onto the rocks there, down to the riverbed. Be very careful when we reach the other side. It would be easy to slip and I don't want any of the horses hurt.'

The patrol began the climb up the hill. It was very still and quiet, as if all the world was at peace. But suddenly the silence was broken by a wild roar. From the shelter of the rocks a gang of horsemen appeared, waving swords and axes and yelling curses on Sir Richard and his soldiers.

When Maude, who had crept from the castle and quietly borrowed one of the faster ponies from the stable, caught up with the patrol, she stopped her pony at the bottom of the hill and gazed in horror at what she saw. The gold of the gorse bushes was spattered with blood and the bodies of men and cattle lay scattered over the hillside. The grey rocks had hidden a raiding party of Mac Conmaras and though the Normans had outnumbered the Irish, the battle had been fierce. It was still going on. Steel met steel and rang out. Steel met flesh and sliced through it. Riderless horses raced around in panic, causing even more confusion. Men and beasts screamed as they were driven over the side of the hill, falling to their death on the rocks in the ravine below.

Through the chaos of shouts and cries, Maude frantically tried to hear Matthieu's voice. She could not see him anywhere. But there was his horse, riderless, fleeing home towards the west. Her heart stopped. Where was her brother? If he has been hurt, I'll kill whoever did it, she thought fiercely, and with a wild cry she urged her horse into the heart of the fighting. But even as she did so, she saw that the Irish were beginning to retreat. Their wild hair was streaming out behind them, and they were moving away from the Normans, calling out to one another in the barbarous language Maude had never tried to understand. She fitted an arrow into her bow and took aim; but the rustlers had disappeared into the shelter of the forest to the north of the hill, and the trees muffled their cries. Sir Richard, unhorsed, stood with his sword in his hand, looking after them with a terrible expression on his face. Maude ran to him.

'Where is Matthieu?' she screamed. 'What's happened to my brother?'

Sir Richard ignored her. He made his way to where his horse lay panting on the ground. Beauvallet's fine black coat was covered in a sheen of sweat and harsh breaths came from his throat. As she looked, Maude realised in horror that the animal's legs were broken. Sir Richard knelt and rubbed the horse's forehead gently.

He said quietly, 'Sleep now, Beauvallet, best of friends.'

Then he walked away and nodded to Fat John, who sent a merciful arrow through Beauvallet's heart.

Maude was standing still, trying to force her legs to take

her to the edge of the ravine to look down to where the river flowed. She knew she had to see if Matthieu's body lay down there with the others who had fallen. But she couldn't move. She stood there, hoping she was not going to be sick, trying to force her legs forward. Let me not fall over, she thought, let them not see my fear.

'Holloa!' Matthieu appeared out from under a gorse bush. He had done his best to fight, waving his sword and shouting at the top of his voice, but the Irish had ignored him. Knocked off his horse in collision with one of Sir Richard's own soldiers, he had rolled under the bush, and kept as quiet as possible while the battle raged on around him.

Maude ran to him and hugged him furiously. She held on so long Matthieu began to protest and tried to free himself. Then he realised that his sister was holding on because she was afraid her legs were going to give way underneath her.

Fat John had surveyed the battlefield and now reported back to Sir Richard.

'One dead – young Patrick, the miller's nephew – and four wounded, two badly. Ten of the cattle dead. Three of the horses. Five of the Irish killed, all of them of the western Mac Conmara clan, by the look of them. There is still one of them alive over there, wounded. What do you want me to do with him?'

'Kill him. Throw him with the other bodies into the ravine. Then strip them all of anything of value they may have on them. Take their horses.' Sir Richard spoke abruptly. 'Then get our wounded onto the horses and we will make our way back. Leave two men to drive the cattle to safety and two to dig a grave for Beauvallet. I would not have his body left for whatever comes from the woods to desecrate it. I swear to you, John, the Mac Conmaras will rue this day.'

Maude looked around her at the scene of carnage. Cows lay with their necks ripped open. Men's bodies lay in positions they could never have taken in life, legs bent underneath their bodies, their heads dangling to one side. There was blood everywhere. The smell of it made her want to throw up. There was no sign of Patrick – his body lay twisted on the rocks in the shallow river bed. Patrick had been tow-headed and tongue-tied, but a wonderful archer. He had often helped Maude when she was practising. And Beauvallet, noble Beauvallet, lay still now, his dark eyes filmed with death. Maude realised that this was not an adventure. This was a nightmare.

And as the silent procession made its way home, something else struck her. The Mac Conmara clan had killed Sir Richard's man and his favourite horse, and they had made war on Sir Richard's soldiers. The truce with the clan was broken. What would happen to Tuan?

PART II

ESCAPE FROM BUNRATTY

CHAPTER 13

Tuan

he day after these events, life in Bunratty suddenly changed. Even the air seemed to become harsher, colder. It was no longer a place where people lived ordinary lives, but a barracks preparing for battle. Lady Johanna, thin-lipped and sharp-tongued, gave orders to start gathering in as much food as possible, in case they should be put under siege. There had been sieges at the castle before now, and for once Lady Johanna unbent enough to talk to Maude about them.

'Sieges are dreadful. The waiting that goes on and on, the hunger, the sickness caused by the lack of fresh water and fresh air. And the boredom. The terrible fights that break out between people who have been cooped up together day after day, sometimes for months. I have seen people go mad during sieges.'

Margaret too looked deeply unhappy, more unhappy than Cliar had ever seen her. She remembered more than one siege at Bunratty; she had lost a husband to one and her parents to another. Her only consolation was that summer was coming.

'At least the cows have started giving more milk now that there's more grass, and we can start the cheesemaking. And there have been good catches of fish down in the Shannon. Cliar, you can start salting the load that Marcus brought in this morning.'

Cliar sighed. This was a job she hated, gutting the fish and placing them between layers of salt in big wooden barrels. Her arms would sting from the salt for days and, even worse, she could not get rid of the smell of fish from her skin and clothes. She would even go swimming in the icy Shannon to try to remove the smell, but it didn't work. Maude had given her some scented soap, and that helped a little. After two hours of gutting and salting, she had more than enough. Tuan, coming to look for her in the kitchen, found her crying as she pulled the slimy red innards into piles and flung them onto the dung heap. Flies had gathered around her and she waved them away angrily.

'I hate this kitchen,' she said, and Tuan realised that he had never heard her sound so angry. 'It's like being in hell. One day I'll just run away from here. I don't care what happens to me, but at least I won't have to gut another fish or chop another onion.'

'Dump those and come with me to the roof,' said Tuan. 'Quick, before anyone sees. Maude has some news for us.'

Maude indeed had news, and she told her tale with a white, shocked face. The worst had happened.

✳ ✳ ✳

Maude had been alone in her chamber with Gile. Because of her flight from the castle she was in disgrace and had been told to help Margaret with packing away valuables into the chests of the Great Hall. But instead she had sneaked back upstairs and was lying in a shaft of sunlight with a very contented dog. Gile was snoring slightly with his paws in the air while she quietly deloused him. She heard a noise on the other side of the thin partition; Sir Richard had come into his chamber to talk privately to Lady Johanna.

Maude listened intently. Sir Richard was speaking in Latin. She knew by experience that when her guardians spoke Latin, they wished to keep what they were saying as secret as possible. Maude's Latin, thought not as good as Matthieu's, was good enough to follow most of their conversation. At first they talked about the attacks to the north of Bunratty, but then she heard Tuan's name mentioned and her ears strained even harder to hear what was being said.

'It will be a pity to harm the child, for he's a good enough boy. But nothing else can be done; the Mac Conmaras must be taught that they cannot take me for a fool.' Sir Richard's voice was harsh.

'That's true enough,' said Lady Johanna. 'But how are we to do it? We cannot do anything in the castle, for he is well liked and there would be uproar from the children and the servants. You must do it quietly and quickly, away from Bunratty.'

'That I know,' said Lord De Clare. 'It is better that I should not be here when it is done, so once I have left for Dysert O'Dea, Fat John will take the child out of the castle. He will make up some story about meeting his family, of returning him to them. He will do what is necessary; hit him from behind like a dog when his mind is elsewhere. Then he can send his son Godric with the body to lay it out where it will be found by the Mac Conmaras, somewhere on the borders of their land. That will teach them to have respect for me again.'

Lady Johanna sighed. 'And when will this be?'

'I leave tomorrow at dawn. After I have left, Fat John will take him away. Then he will continue south to tell Prior Outlaw to join me at Dysert.'

'And you do not think Tuan will be suspicious? There is no love between him and Fat John.'

'I think not, but if he is, Fat John will drug him and carry him out of the castle over his saddle.'

Maude put her hand over her mouth. She was shaking as if with cold, although the sun still beamed through the window. She could not believe that her guardians were planning to kill Tuan. Even if it were true that the Mac Conmara clan had broken the truce, Tuan himself had done nothing. Nor had his parents, who had made the agreement with Sir Richard.

She tried to think straight. Tuan had to get out of the castle tonight. But how this could be done was, thought Maude gloomily, a different matter altogether.

But Lady Johanna and Sir Richard had not finished their conversation.

'On another matter,' said Sir Richard. 'You know that De Burgh has a young nephew, the same age as Maude?'

'I had heard so, but I have never met him; your alliance with De Burgh is so recent.'

'So it is, and still fragile. I have thought of a way to make it stronger. As we have no daughter of our own, do you think it might serve us well to marry Maude to him? She is young, but girls her age have been married before now, and she is of no use to you here in the castle.'

For once, Lady Johanna sounded quite cheerful. 'Faith, I would be glad to see the back of her. Especially after her latest romp. It is a pity the De Burghs are not here tonight for the dancing. What is the De Burgh boy like?'

'Quite ugly and very stupid, as far as I can remember, but does that matter?'

'Not at all,' said Lady Johanna.

They both laughed as they left the room.

Maude sat biting her lip. So she was to be sold off to strengthen Sir Richard's alliances. But more serious than that threat was the danger to Tuan. She had to warn him. She had to warn him even though her code of honour meant that her loyalty was to her lord, to Sir Richard, not to a boy she would once have described as an Irish savage. But the Irish savage was now her good friend. Perhaps the code of knighthood was not always right?

Maude buried her face in Gile's fur, thinking hard. Was that possible? Ever since she could remember, Maude had listened to her father talk about the code, how it made the Normans different from everyone else. Made them better. She had desperately wanted to be a knight herself. It had made her so angry that Matthieu was the one who was given training in the use of arms. One day he would be raised to the rank of Sir Matthieu and be allowed out into the world to make his fortune and have adventures. She would be stuck behind the walls of some castle, no doubt married to some awful husband. She would have to listen to everything he said and pretend to be interested. She would have to obey him, even if he was someone stupid and cruel. She would have nothing to do but look after the kitchen and have babies and sew and say her prayers. And it seemed that this fate awaited her very soon, in the form of De Burgh's stupid and ugly nephew. The thought of it made her want to spit. No, that was not the life she wanted.

But did she really want to be a knight either, now that she had seen the battle on the hillside? What she had seen there had made her wonder about how much chivalry or honour there really was in battle. Blood everywhere and men's bodies broken so that they screamed out in agony?

It had little grace about it.

She shook her head to clear the thoughts away. She was wasting time. She was not someone who went through agonies about what to do before she acted. And although this trait often got her into trouble, in a crisis it was her strength. Think about what to do *now,* she told herself. It was simple, really: Tuan was her friend. She would have to get him out of the castle and away from Bunratty somehow, and as quickly as possible.

She stood up as Matthieu came into the chamber. At first he did not notice that Maude had been crying. When he saw how upset she was, he went over to her and gave her a hug.

'What is it?' he asked. For once she did not shake him off, but hugged him back.

'I overheard something,' she whispered. 'They're planning to kill Tuan.'

Matthieu's mouth opened in shock. Tuan? Tuan, who was kind; Tuan who didn't tease him; Tuan who tried to help him with his sword-play and archery without making him feel stupid, as Maude did?

'Who – who is planning it?' he asked. 'Are you sure?'

'I heard Sir Richard and Lady Johanna talking about it,' said Maude. 'It's true.'

Matthieu started to cry.

I should have known better, thought Maude. Matthieu was still a baby, and though she loved him dearly and would have protected him with her life, she could not really depend on him to help. Cry, yes; help, no.

Matthieu caught her look and wiped his eyes. 'I'm sorry. Look, I've stopped. But we have to save him, don't we? We have to get him to safety, like we did with the stag. Cliar will help, and Dame Anna. Can we go and tell Tuan and Cliar what's happening?'

Maude nodded. 'Yes, we have to act quickly. Fat John is going to take him away from the castle tomorrow!'

✳ ✳ ✳

When the four children met on the roof, Maude, despite knowing exactly what she wanted to say, found it hard to start. She suddenly realised that she didn't know how to tell Tuan that he was going to be killed.

'I overheard Lady Johanna and Sir Richard talking ...' she began, then stopped.

Matthieu burst out: 'They're plotting to kill Tuan. It's because of what happened with the Mac Conmaras.'

'But that's not my father's family!' said Tuan angrily. 'They're distant cousins, yes, but it is not my father who attacked! He has not broken his promise!'

'That doesn't seem to matter to Sir Richard. He is really angry about the raid – and especially about poor Beauvallet. Anyway, *he* has broken *his* promise before now. And look at his father.'

Everyone thought of Brian Rua, dragged out from feasting and savagely killed by Thomas De Clare.

Tuan felt his anger rise. How dare they? How dare the Norman English walk all over his people, killing them and taking their lands? The lands that this very castle stood on had once been Mac Conmara lands, his people's lands. Bunratty castle should not be here at all. Tuan suddenly realised how much he hated being in the castle, living in the enclosed, dark space. It was true that the halls and huts his people lived in were dark and smoky too, but they spent so little time inside them that it hardly mattered. Bunratty smelt bad, he thought, it smelt of blood and it smelt of burning. Its walls were a prison.

'I will kill De Clare myself,' he said.

'Yes, and end up dead with your head decorating the castle walls like one of the deer from the forest. Though without the antlers,' Maude snapped.

Cliar said slowly, 'Well ... it looks like De Clare himself

may be killed in any case.'

'What?' Tuan, Maude and Matthieu all spoke together.

She told them about Sir Richard's visit to Dame Anna. 'She said something about getting a message to Outlaw. If we go to her, maybe she can tell us how to rescue Tuan and get word to the Prior at the same time. I tried to talk to her earlier, but she was so busy with the wounded there was no time. And now she has gone back into her tower and when I tried to open the door, it was locked. That's never happened before.'

'I can try to fight Fat John and Godric when they take me away from the castle,' said Tuan. 'At least I know what to expect now.'

'Fat John and Godric? You wouldn't have a hope.' Maude's voice was scornful. 'No, the only thing to do is to get away from the castle before tomorrow. And I have an idea how we can do it. But then we have to decide what to do with you when you do get out. It's too dangerous for you to try to get back to your clan. There are English and Scottish armies everywhere east of Cratloe. What we should do is go to Prior Roger in Knockainy. He said he would help you get back to your people safely. And that way we can warn him of what's happening, and tell him not to follow

Sir Richard to Dysert O'Dea.'

Tuan looked at Maude. He had already begun to imagine his escape, taking off back home to the hills and the forest. Back to his own people. But he knew the chances of making it even as far as Cratloe were very faint. Soldiers always shot on sight and asked questions later. Maude's plan made sense. You had to admit it, she'd thought of everything.

'It is true that the woods to the east are full of soldiers,' he said. 'But even if I do try to get to Outlaw, first I have to get out of the castle. And that's my biggest problem.'

'Not exactly,' said Maude. 'The problem is that *we* have to get out of the castle. Matthieu and I are coming with you.'

Matthieu looked as if this was news to him too, but said nothing.

'Why on earth would you do that?' said Tuan. 'You'll be safe here.'

'I wouldn't be too sure about that. We could end up burnt to death or stuck here in a siege. Listen, I've been thinking hard and imagining being stuck with Lady Johanna for months if there's a siege … if I had to listen to her for that length of time I would probably end up killing her. Or myself. Or burning the castle down or something equally dreadful. And on top of that they're talking about marrying me off to some horrible De Burgh ally. This *cannot* happen! If we get to Prior Outlaw, perhaps he can help me and Matthieu get some news of our father. And if we all travel together it will make it easier for you, too. When we're on the road, if we meet any English soldiers we can say you're our servant.'

'I bet you would only love that,' muttered Tuan. He was not at all sure he wanted to go on this adventure with Maude. He knew she would try to boss everyone. She couldn't help it. But then, at the same time he had to admit that it would be nice to have company. He looked at Cliar. If only she was coming too.

'I'm coming too,' said Cliar. 'I'm not going to be left behind here. I wasn't born when the last siege was on, but Margaret has told me all about it. It was awful. Nearly every living thing was sick; humans and animals and even the birds. When the sick animals died they were catapulted from the battlements to get them out of the castle and to try to spread disease among the attackers. But the Irish catapulted them right back. And I do remember bits about the battle here seven years ago. It was horrible – there were bodies everywhere; they buried them in big pits because there were so many. And then just a couple of years later the village was burnt and lots of the settlers driven out. I'll never forget the smell of burning ... I am not going to wait here and see it all happen again.'

She smiled, a little shakily. 'And anyway, you are the first real friends I have ever had, friends of my own age, and I'm not going to watch you go off while I'm stuck behind in Bunratty.'

Maude hugged her. 'So, it's decided. Lady Johanna has organised some musicians to come tonight and there will be dancing and feasting. All we have to do is get past the sentries and take a boat down the Ratty to the Shannon. I know where there's some rope, so we can climb over the battlements while the sentry is patrolling the other side. In any case, they won't be watching for people getting *out*, but for people trying to get *in*. Once we get out we can cross the Shannon in the boat and take to the fields on the other side.'

Tuan shook his head. 'We'd be better to stay with the boat. Remember what Outlaw said. There's a river that feeds into the Shannon from the other side – the Maigue. If we find it, we can follow it down towards Knockainy.' Tuan was trying hard to remember the rest of Prior Outlaw's directions. But while he remembered the bit about following the Maigue, the rest of what the Prior had said was a blur in his head. He knew they had to leave the river at some point, but when? It would come back to him somehow. He hoped.

CHAPTER 14

Escape

 hat night in the Great Hall the dancing failed to cheer anyone up. The dancers went through the motions, aware that Lady Johanna was watching and would be displeased if her efforts at entertainment were not appreciated. Sir Richard sat with a frown on his face, cursing his servants for being too slow to serve him and lashing out at Lady Johanna when she asked him what the matter was. Cliar was careful to keep as far away as possible from him as she served the meat and wine. She did not want to remind him that she had been there when Dame Anna had seen disaster ahead of him. Nor did she want anyone to notice her red eyes.

Cliar had been crying all day, pretending to Margaret that she had a cold so that she would not question her too closely. She had told her that Dame Anna wanted her help after the feast so that Margaret would not wonder why she was not in her bed that night. Before going down to serve in the Great Hall she had hugged Margaret tightly, but Margaret, busy and overworked as always, had pushed her away impatiently, saying: 'Get on with you – the sooner you're gone the sooner you'll be back to help me. I know we'll need Dame Anna's lotions and powders in the future, but God knows she could have chosen some other time to ask for you. I'm worn out and I could have done with you to help with the clearing up after the feasting.'

But the ghosts were not so easily fooled, and there had been a lot of wailing in the castle, for the word had gone around that Cliar was leaving. After she had said a tearful goodbye to them, she made one last attempt to enter the tower, but the door would not budge. If she's in there, at least she'll be able to see us in her silver bowl, Cliar thought, but somehow the thought brought no consolation.

Matthieu watched the dancing, tired and stiff and sore from his fall and still feeling slightly sick from all he had seen that day. But the bright colours moving in the shadows and the sound of the music put him into a kind of trance and helped him not to think about the horror. It made him imagine a world without tourneys and battles. Why did people have to fight all the time? Was it because they felt they needed to win? Everyone was like that, even the children in the village, playing that game they spent all their time at. It was an Irish game, requiring great skill. There was a blown up pig's bladder that opposing teams tried to hit into the space between two hurdles – they called it the goal. They hit it with a stick, although sometimes the children ended up just kicking it from one to another. If all the knights in the world were to kick around a stuffed pig's bladder and try to get it into a goal made of wattles, maybe, thought Matthieu, that would get rid of the need they had to fight and win. To triumph over someone. He smiled to himself at the thought of it.

Then he wondered if other people had such strange thoughts. He told nobody about them, because he knew he would only be laughed at. Nobody laughed at Maude; everyone listened to her because she sounded so passionate about what she said, and her ideas were always practical and clear, not like his. He was passionate too, about his dreams, but nobody seemed to realise it or indeed to listen to him at all. Sometimes Matthieu felt he was no more than a reflection of the stronger characters that surrounded him. There were times he felt he might as well be invisible, for he seemed to have no effect on all the events that were happening around him. Even Maude, much as he loved her and she loved him, sometimes seemed not to be aware that he was there. He had talked to Cliar about this and she had known exactly what he was talking about. 'It's the same with me,' she said. 'I'm only a servant, so people don't notice me. But remember, Matthieu, that can be very useful sometimes; you can hear things and see things that others might not be allowed to hear. Remember that.'

Like birds, thought Matthieu. Nobody minded if a pigeon sat on a windowsill beside them as they shared secrets with each other. Yet here in the castle they so often looked as if they were listening, their head cocked to one side; and then they would fly to the tower, into Dame Anna's window, for whatever titbits she could give them – or perhaps that they could give her? He was brought back to reality by a sharp thump on his shoulder from Maude.

'Wake up! Now is our chance while the dancing is on,' she whispered in his ear. 'I've told Cliar to get Tuan and meet us in the hayloft. The roof is too dangerous with all the sentries. Come, let's go upstairs and get our cloaks and Gile. Be quick now. And take some bread and meat from the table, we'll need food for the journey.'

Even in the warmth of the hayloft, Cliar and Tuan were shivering as they waited for the other two. The night was clear and very cold. Tuan had not gone to the Great Hall that night, as he felt that if he saw Sir Richard he would not be able to keep his fury from showing. He had found himself, as the evening went on and he sat in his little room, getting angrier and angrier. Tuan thought of his cousins – all soldiers, both boys and girls – riding over the wild hills, hair flowing, roaring at the tops of their voices, or taking the boats out onto the ocean, with the sun streaming on the water and the call of the gulls urging them to go faster, faster, to challenge the rocks and the waves and the wind with their speed and strength. He should be with them, not caught like a fly in De Clare's spider's web. He wanted to see his own people; he wanted to be home, sleeping around the fire with his cousins in the warmth of the hall, not in this cold, stone, stinking place.

He thought of his beloved mother. She would be praying for him, as she had promised to do every morning and every night. She had given him a hare's paw to keep him safe; a lucky talisman. He wondered if it had been her prayers or the lucky talisman that had kept him safe so far. He also wondered how long such luck would last.

He dozed off and woke abruptly to Cliar shaking him.

'Come quickly,' she said. 'We have to meet the others in the hayloft.'

The cock crowed and Tuan said: 'He never shuts up. If I could do just one thing before I leave the castle to make me happy, it would be to strangle that cock and set him to boil in a pot of herbs.'

Cliar laughed as she led him away.

The four children and Gile made themselves comfortable high up on some baled straw. The barn was mostly bare now of winter fodder, but they were hidden and secret in the hayloft.

Maude flicked back her hair and Tuan couldn't help but smile – it was such a girly gesture for a tomboy. She caught him smiling and grimaced at him.

'So, this is the plan,' she announced. 'I have got the rope we need to get down the walls on the other side of the battlements. The only problem is Godric – he's on duty tonight and if he sees us we're in trouble. We must try to get over the wall while he's patrolling the other side of the roof. It's a cloudy night, so let's wait until the moon is hidden. There will be less chance of being seen.'

The children sat in the darkness, all of them feeling slightly sick at what lay ahead of them. If they were caught there would be no second chance for Tuan to escape from death. It seemed like a long time to wait, but finally the moon went behind a cloud and Maude sprang up.

'Let's go, fast.'

The four children and the dog scrambled towards the stairs which led to the roof. But at the top they stopped in their tracks, for standing on the battlements, looking over towards them, was Godric.

'Hell's curses on him,' whispered Maude. He had spotted them and raised his lantern towards them. The moon, which had been hidden, had suddenly come out from behind the clouds.

'And what are you doing here, might I ask?' he said. But as he spoke, there was a rustling in the air and a cloud of silver swept across from Dame Anna's window. A flock of doves circled Godric and he shouted angrily as the children hastily lowered the rope over the edge of the battlements.

'Tighten it there as much as you can, Tuan,' whispered Maude, as Tuan attached the rope to one of the crennelations. 'You go first, Matthieu. Then Cliar.'

Matthieu looked down. It was a very long way to the

ground. But there was no time to lose. Godric was still bat-
tling with the white cloud, but how long could the birds
keep him at bay?

The watchers on the roof heard Matthieu land with a
thump and a cry of protest on the soft turf at the bottom of
the wall.

'Cliar, you next,' said Maude.

But Cliar paused, for she had seen something. Godric
had raised his bow and shot one of the birds as it circled
him. She saw it fall; and the figure inside the circling birds
lifted his bow in triumph.

'It's wounded,' she said. 'I must bring it to Dame Anna.
You go on,' she said frantically. 'I'll follow you, don't
worry. I'll meet you by the boat at the jetty.'

Tuan paused and seemed as if he was about to argue, but
Maude pushed him roughly towards the rope. If Tuan was
caught he would die.

'Take Gile,' she said. 'And hold onto him tightly, he
weighs a ton.'

Tuan and then Maude slid down the rope. But Cliar ran
towards where the bird had fallen to the ground and caught
it in her hands. Holding it as gently as she could, she rushed
down the staircase, and ran as fast as she was able towards

the north west tower, Godric calling angrily behind her, 'Come back! I hit it, it's mine!'

She paid no heed. She caught her breath in relief when the door of the tower opened. Slamming it behind her, she raced up the stairs and into Dame Anna's chamber. But when she entered, the room seemed empty. The fire was out, a pile of dull, grey ashes. Dame Anna was not at her spinning wheel, nor mixing her potions. Cliar looked around; surely Dame Anna could not have left Bunratty?

Then she saw the cloaked figure lying at the edge of the dead fire. It was Dame Anna, and for one horrible moment Cliar thought that she was dead. But she realised that the woman was only sleeping, for her breath, though shallow, was regular. Cliar looked down at the bird she was holding in her hands, the black arrow still piercing its feathers, red blood staining the whiteness. No heart-beat. It was already dead.

For the first time Cliar looked into Dame Anna's face and realised how very old she was. It shook her; she had never thought of her as an old, frail lady. Should she wake her? No. There was no time. She laid the bird gently in the ashes of the fire and made her way downstairs. Godric had disappeared. Had he gone to raise the alarm? Cliar raced to where the rope still hung down the wall. Brian Rua was standing there.

'Don't worry about Godric,' he said. 'Them white pigeons have given him a fair pecking and have addled what little wits he has, fluttering around him. And some of us helped – we did a few apparitions and flapped around him, and he took off, scared, muttering about pigeons and children and some kind of stag coming for him. Fat John has sent him to bed to sleep it off. But you must hurry – another sentry is on the way.'

Cliar gave the ghost a grateful smile, but there was no time to waste with more discussion. She had to join the others. She climbed onto the wall and down the rope, out of Bunratty.

At the jetty the others were waiting impatiently. Tuan had chosen a small blue rowing boat that would just about fit the four children and Gile, and would be light enough for them to drag along if there were stretches of the river which were too shallow for them to sail on.

They piled in and Tuan took the oars. 'Have any of you ever rowed a boat before?' he asked the others.

Maude and Matthieu shook their heads. There had always been a servant to row them wherever they needed to go.

'It looks easy, though,' said Maude.

'It's not as easy as it looks,' said Tuan. 'I'll do the rowing until we get well out into the Shannon. Anyway, it will be quicker.'

'I can row,' said Cliar. 'Do you want me to take the oars for a while?'

Tuan shook his head. 'No, let me get us out a bit from the land first. After that we can take it in turns.'

As they made their way across the river, Tuan remembered his arrival in the castle. Another moon now, and a sky full of scudding clouds. He looked into the trees and wondered if he had actually caught a glimpse back then of the Silver Stag in the darkness. Would he ever see it again?

There was a cold wind from the water as they made their way across the Shannon. There were no other boats on the river. Even during the daytime, there were less boats on the river than usual, for no-one travelled now unless they had to. There was danger everywhere. The countryside was full of English patrols and Irish raiding parties. Anyone who had a home with walls was taking refuge behind them and hoping that the trouble would soon die down. Stories came from the north of burning villages and captives taken.

Matthieu was shivering and Cliar smiled at him.

'It could be worse,' she said. 'It could be January.'

Maude sniffed. 'Where we come from, January is warmer than this.'

Tuan, already tired with rowing four children and a dog against the strong current of the Shannon, said: 'Oh please, could you stop telling us how wonderful it is where you come from and how dreadful it is here? Here is where we are, let's just get on with it.'

Matthieu said quietly: 'And you know, Maude, in May it would be starting to get really hot, and do you remember how awful it was in July and August? How it was impossible to go out in the middle of the day because of the sun? How fed up you used to get being stuck in for hours and the trouble you got into the times you escaped and went out without permission? I think I prefer the rain!'

'That's all right then, you gang up with the Irish!' Maude huddled down with Gile held tight in her arms.

Cliar opened her mouth to say something, then snapped it shut. There was silence. All of them wondered if leaving Bunratty together had really been such a good idea.

✳ ✳ ✳

I wish I knew where I was going, thought Tuan. I am the one who has to lead the group – no-one else knows anything about boats or being on the water – though Cliar at least knew how to handle the oars and had done it without fuss. Matthieu, on the other hand, had been so slow and careful when he began that he drove Tuan mad, but after a while he managed quite well. Maude, impatient and unable to take any advice, was worst of all. She almost lost an oar when she flung it away in a temper after Tuan tried to show her how to stop the boat going around in circles. After this, realising that she had almost destroyed their chances of escape, Maude was quieter, but it was painful to watch her rowing, her anger and frustration at being unable to do something she thought simple was so obvious.

'Sure, how would you know how to row a boat and you living in the desert?' teased Tuan, hoping to make her feel better, but all he got in return was a furious look. Soon all their hands, even Tuan's, were red and blistered from the oars. Tuan wondered how far they would get, at the rate they were going. At least they did not have to go along the Shannon as far as Limerick town, which was full of soldiers and bridges. Four children and a dog in a boat would not have got through at all easily.

'There's the Maigue!' Tuan pointed, and Cliar, who was rowing, began the approach to the smaller river that flowed from the south into the Shannon.

'Can't we go faster now?' said Maude impatiently. 'Surely it must be easier on the smaller river?'

Tuan made a face. 'It's still tidal so it's still very hard work.'

Maude said nothing else but gave Cliar an apologetic glance.

They were afraid to stop, wanting to put as much distance as possible between themselves and the Bunratty patrols. By the time the day was beginning to dawn, all of the children were cold, wet and miserable. They finally came to a spot in the river where it widened out into a pleasant meadow and some sheltering beeches grew on the west bank.

'Let's stop for a while,' said Cliar. 'We must be miles from Bunratty now.'

All of them were still grumpy, and when Tuan tried to organise their tasks for making camp, Maude spat angry words at him, asking him what made him think he was in charge.

Cliar decided she had had enough. 'For pity's sake, let's save our energy for making a fire and putting up branches to make some kind of shelter. Maude, will you help me with the fire if Matthieu and Tuan collect the branches?'

Maude had the grace to look a little shamefaced, though she did not go so far as to apologise to Tuan. When they had built a shelter of branches and the fire was roaring, and they were drinking the soup and chewing on the bread that Cliar had filched from the kitchen, they all felt a lot better.

The fire had long gone out when they woke up late in the afternoon, stiff and sore. They were all very silent as they packed up. Then Matthieu, who was looking at his hands in dismay, said dolefully: 'I don't think I'm going to be able to row very well.' His hands were a mass of blisters.

Maude's were no better, so Cliar took out some of her precious salve and rubbed it on all of them. 'I should have thought of this earlier,' she said. 'It takes a while to work.'

Progress along the river was slower because of the children's sore hands. The banks were no longer edged with fields and farms and grazing cattle, but with thick forest and, at times, with marshlands where birds flew out, frightened by the plash of the oars and Gile's excited barking.

Maude, half asleep in the prow, thought how much she hated these Irish forests. All this confusion and brambles and hidden ways. How she longed for the wide view, the sky and the air of the desert. She dreamed of deserts and mountains and riders with golden shawls protecting their faces from the dry, dusty wind. She would go back, she swore to herself, she would go back to the lands of the east one day and find her father. Or at least find out what had happened to him. She would have so much to tell him.

She shivered; the woods were getting darker. The trees here were evergreens, making a black shade that was much more frightening than the lighter shade of the woods around Bunratty. A green darkness that could hide anything.

And now they had rounded a bend in the river and come to a part of the forest where the trees were somehow different ... darker again, with twisted, evil shapes. Stories she had heard in the castle started to drift through her head ... wild animals like wolves – and worse, the people who had taken to the wild woods south of the Shannon, the outlaws and the murderers and the landless and masterless men who lived outside normal laws, normal ways of being. In these desperate times, it was said that some of them even ate humans ...

Cliar's mind was also on the stories of the wild men of the forest. She tried hard not to remember Janet's grisly tales. She was still worried by the memory of how pale Dame Anna had been, fast asleep by the dead fire. She also wondered if she was really ready to leave the castle, the only home she had ever known, with its familiar sounds and smells and the safety of its walls. But if she had stayed, what would her future have been? Dame Anna might well leave the castle, and Margaret would not understand that Cliar might want more from life than to become a housekeeper like herself. Or marry one of the villagers, like Margaret's own son, Fred. If Maude could find the courage to get away from other people making plans for her, so could she, Cliar felt. But this forest was so dark and so ... so endless. All the kitchen stories came back into her head. The babies who had disappeared from woodcutters' cottages, the children sent for water to a well at the edge of the trees who had never come back to their home ...

Why was there a rustling movement on the left bank of the boat, she wondered? She glanced at Gile, but he did not seem to be alarmed. In fact, he was asleep. But there! There was the movement again. Were they being tracked by some kind of animal? Gile suddenly jumped up and started to bark furiously.

Tuan, who had been resting, took over the oars again, but when he went to take them, he thought he saw something move in the trees on the left bank. A deer, he thought hopefully; or had it been a glimpse of a fox's red brush? If it had, the fox must be the size of a horse, for the brush had been at a man's height. He could feel the hairs on the back of his neck rise, and he glanced around at his companions. All of them looked uneasy, as if they too felt that they were being watched. Yes, there were eyes watching them from the cover of the forest.

'Do you think ...' Matthieu began, but he never got to finish his sentence, for there was a sudden rustling of leaves and the children realised that they were surrounded by the strangest group of men they had ever seen.

CHAPTER 15

FOXFACE

he men stood on either bank of the river, bows drawn, ready to shoot. There were four of them, dressed in filthy and ragged clothes. Their faces were so covered in hair and dirt that it was impossible to tell what age they might be. Anywhere their skin showed through, it was a dark greenish colour, as if they had rubbed plants into it to help them hide in the green of the wood. Their teeth were very white and sharp in their dark faces. One of them, the man who seemed to be the leader, carried no bow but wore animal skins and a belt which held a long knife. He had a fox's pelt draped over his head, its head hanging low over his face with its teeth set in a snarl, the brush hanging down his back. Gile began to growl and the foxman moved forward with his hand raised. He spoke slowly, in English.

'So, this is a fine clutch of young chickens we have here. And where might you be going, all on your lonesome with the evening coming on, in these wild woods?'

Maude stood up, almost upsetting the boat. She said proudly, 'We are journeying up the river to meet our ... our uncle, and it please you.'

'And it may be that it does not please me at all, young maid. Have ye asked permission of Foxface for that? Have they, men?'

He turned to the green-clad archers, all of whom shook their heads and murmured.

'No, ye have not,' said Foxface. 'So what's to do, then?'

'I did not think we needed permission to use the free waterways of this country.' Maude's voice did not falter.

'Oh, ye must pay a fine, everyone must pay a fine who passes through these woods. No one comes here but us; we guard the way. So I'll thank ye to tie up the boat and come with us.'

The children did not move. Gile growled again.

'Now, don't ye be looking like ye might not want to come along the way with us. That wouldn't be nice of ye at all. We'll treat ye gently, my chickens, of course we will. But ye have no hope of getting away from us so ye might as well come quietly. I wouldn't like to see that fine dog of yours shot down in his prime.'

He stared at Gile, who backed up against Maude's legs, whining softly.

Foxface continued: 'So I'll thank you to keep him under control, Mistress. Now, we're going to take a look and see if ye have any knives or suchlike, and then we're going to tie yer hands behind yer backs and loop ye one to another, for fear ye should try to escape. Look to it, men.'

The children exchanged glances, and, without a word, gathered their bundles and got out of the boat. Tuan tied it to a willow, wondering if they would ever see it again. The gang of men surrounded them, opening their bundles and spilling the contents onto the forest floor. Cliar looked on sorrowfully as they emptied the precious bottles of healing medicine. A smell of unwashed flesh and hair and clothes, and an undertone of something else, surrounded the children, blocking out the clear air of the forest. Cliar shivered as she realised what the something else was. It was blood. These men smelt of blood.

They began the march through the forest, going single file. The dense undergrowth, full of nettles and thistles and brambles, and the rough ground underneath did not seem to bother their captors or slow them down in the slightest, but the children found it hard to keep up. Here I go again, thought Tuan, as a bramble snapped back from the path and scratched his face. Will I ever be free? All four children tried hard not to think about the stories of the wild men of the woods, the men who ate any flesh they could capture, even if it was human ...

It seemed like a very long time before they reached a clearing in the wood. Here there were two roughly built huts, thatched with broom and ferns. In the centre was a small fire, smoking lazily. The place was covered in rubbish of every kind – bits of old iron and other metals, rotting vegetables, piles of bones that the children did not like to look at too closely.

Foxface poked the children forward with a stick, closer to the fire, and muttered something to his followers, who now moved forwards to tie their feet together as well as their hands. Gile was tied to a tree. Trussed like chickens, the children looked at each other dolefully.

Maude addressed the Foxman, who was regarding them with a very unpleasant smile. She had decided that politeness might be more useful than defiance.

'My Lord,' she said, 'I have not fully introduced my

companions and myself. This is the Lady Cliar, this is Lord
Tuan, of the Irish clans, this my brother Matthieu FitzHerbert of Outremer. I myself am the Lady Maude. We are
delighted to make your acquaintance.'

Foxface looked at them impassively, and then laughed.
Gile's hackles rose and one of the other men gave him a
vicious kick.

'Pay no attention to my dog, may it please you,' said
Maude. 'He is of a rare and noble breed and is inclined to be
over-protective of us.'

'So, young mistress, what might be yer real reason for
making yer way through the forest? Through *my* forest?
Who gave ye permission?'

Tuan chimed in. 'Dame Anna has sent us on a mission to
give a message to one of her kinsmen. It is important that
we get to him as soon as possible.'

'The Dame Anna, indeed. We would not wish to distress
the Dame Anna. But who is the kinsman you must reach?'

Matthieu said eagerly. 'It is Roger Outlaw, the Prior of
the Hospitallers.'

There came a sound from Foxface; this time it was close
to a growl. 'Ah, Outlaw, who tries to bring his stinking laws
into the woods and who cuts the trees at Ainy to roof his

chapels! I love him not, my chickens, and would as soon see an ill turn done to him as a good one. So I think we will keep ye here with us a little, to see what yer payment for passing through our woods is to be.'

'These are O'Brien lands, not yours,' said Tuan, and the fox mask turned towards him contemptuously.

'Here in the forest neither Irish nor English rule,' Foxface snarled. 'These are no-one's lands, but ours. I'm tired of yer babbling,' he said suddenly. 'Be quiet, chickens, or I'll cut yer tongues out.' He added something that the children could not hear and went into one of the huts with two of the other men. One of his companions was left outside, and he took his place by the fire, watching them, and whittling at a long pole and two pronged supports.

'What do you think they're going to do with us?' whispered Matthieu.

'I don't like the way Foxy Loxy keeps calling us chickens,' whispered Cliar, shuddering. 'And that thing your man is carving looks awfully like a spit. But I can't see any food.'

'Except us,' said Maude dolefully.

'Do you really think they will eat us?' said Matthieu.

'Margaret told me stories about people who have gone so wild in the forest that they actually eat other people,' said

Cliar. 'But I am trying not to believe these are as bad as she made out. Most of the people in the woods are just outlaws that can't live in towns or villages or with any other people – some of them are driven away because they have diseases that people might catch, some of them because the law is after them.'

'Did you get what that word was, the one they kept repeating to each other when they were whispering?' asked Matthieu.

'Yes,' said Tuan. 'I think it was dinner.'

There was a silence after this.

Maude finally spoke. 'I have heard it said that the Irish ate people–'

'It's not the Irish, it's just this crowd,' hissed Tuan. 'And it sounded to me like Mr Fox had an English accent, not an Irish one.'

Cliar sighed. 'Oh, don't start arguing about whether this lot are Irish or English. If they're going to eat us, I don't really care whether it's the Irish way, boiled with kale, or the English one, roasted with parsley sauce … we need to think of a plan to get out of here.'

They sat for several moments in silence, but no plan seemed forthcoming.

Matthieu found his mind drifting. 'Which do you think would be the worst? To be boiled or roasted?'

Maude had been thinking hard. It would be up to her, she thought, to get them out of this mess. She snapped at her brother: 'Oh Matthieu, will you shut up. You got us into enough trouble with your mention of Outlaw.'

Cliar smiled at him as he fought back tears. 'Don't worry about it, Matthieu. They probably won't bother cooking us at all.'

The children lay in silence, and after a while the other men came out of the hut. They looked as if they had been drinking, and two of them, the foxman and the tallest of the others, carried large, empty jugs.

'You stay here, Ru, with Buna, and we'll bring back more drink for the feast. There are some fat monks further down the river whose cellar is only waiting to be raided.'

Neither Ru nor Buna looked too happy at this plan, but said nothing.

When Foxface and the other man had gone, Ru, who looked a little the worse for his drinking, began to shift around restlessly and kicked at the fire, muttering.

'What's wrong with you?' asked the other.

At this stage, Matthieu, who had been wriggling around

uncomfortably for some time, spoke up: 'Excuse me, sirs, do you think you could help me here?'

Oh no, thought Maude, please, please don't walk yourself into more trouble, Matthieu. I told you to shut up.

But it was too late, and she watched in horror as Ru went over and pulled Matthieu up roughly.

'A small one, but noisy,' he said, then he lifted him bodily and, to horrified gasps from the children, threw him in the air towards his companion.

'Catch as catch can!' he shouted, but Matthieu fell with a thump to the ground, and cried out with pain. Gile began to bark, frantically trying to free himself from his leash.

The other man went over to Matthieu and picked him up again. 'Here, you try this time,' he said.

'Please, please, don't,' Maude was calling out, tears in her eyes.

But the men ignored her, and now Buna had stumbled towards Matthieu and lifted him again. He swung him towards Ru.

The other children shut their eyes, waiting in horror for the thump on the ground and another cry of pain from Matthieu.

But the cry of pain was from Ru, for Matthieu had not

only head-butted him as he reached his tormentor, but was now hanging out of his long, greasy hair and scrabbling in his captor's belt for his knife.

'Tuan, catch!' he shouted, and Tuan rolled over and, though he didn't manage to catch the knife, got close enough to it to pick it up between his bound hands and slash open Cliar's bonds. As soon as her hands were free, she cut free Tuan's hands and feet, and then went quickly on to Maude and Gile.

The four of them headed like a swarm of bees onto the heaving mass that was Ru, Buna and Matthieu. They bit, scratched and kicked until the men let go; Maude hung out of Ru's back like a monkey, thumping him as hard as she could and shouting at him, 'You dare hurt my brother, you dare!' Cliar pulled a stick from the fire and, using the lighted end, managed to set alight Buna's clothes. Tuan, who now had the knife, waved it at both men and shouted at them to get away or he would put it through their hearts. Gile nipped at whatever piece of arm or leg was closest to him, drawing yowls of pain from the two outlaws.

Finally, Maude hit Ru over the head with the tinderbox and he fell to his knees; Buna was rolling on the ground, trying to put out the flames in his clothes. The children ran for the trees, but before they did, Cliar, for good measure, threw a flaming branch from the fire at the hut and set it blazing.

They could hear shouts and growls behind them and the crackle of flames; but they did not look back, they just kept running through the wood. It felt like hours later that they bundled themselves into a hole in a bank. It was big enough to hold them all, and seemed to be an animal's lair, smelling strongly of some kind of wild beast.

'The smell will cover our scent from them,' said Tuan, between gasps for air. 'We should be safe here until morning.'

'Oh Matthieu, you're bleeding,' said Maude.

Matthieu's wrists were indeed bleeding, though not heavily. He was also already developing some very colourful bruises from having been thrown onto the ground of the clearing. In fact, he looked a complete mess. But he grinned.

'I think I must have cut myself when I was rubbing the ropes to get free. You see, there was an old piece of metal with a sharp edge to it where they threw me on the ground when we arrived. That's how I managed to cut through the rope.'

Maude hugged him. 'You were very brave. And clever. That's why you tried to get their attention, wasn't it, to get them near you?'

Matthieu nodded.

Cliar looked at the wound and then crawled out of their hiding place and collected some moss to bind the red, angry wounds. She also found fresh water, that had gathered in the roots at the base of a tree, in which to soak the moss.

'I just hope the metal was not too dirty or rusty,' she said when she got back. 'If only I still had my potions! And your bruises, look at them. That fall must really have hurt.'

Matthieu grinned again. 'Well, at least I'm well used to falling on the ground!' he said. 'I do it all the time during tourney practice!'

But later that evening they realised that it was not the fall that would cause Matthieu problems.

'Maude, Maude!'

'I'm here, Matthieu, don't worry.'

'Why is Maman here, Maude? And Papa too?'

Maude went pale. Matthieu was shifting restlessly. Even in the darkness the others could see that his face was scarlet, feverish.

Cliar leaned over and felt his forehead. 'He's burning up.

He's got a bad fever. It must be from some poison on the metal he cut himself on.'

'What can we do?' Maude asked.

Tuan realised that had never heard Maude sound frightened before.

'We must try to keep him cool and comfortable, and hope the fever breaks,' explained Cliar. 'If only Dame Anna was here!' She did not want to admit to the others how frightened she was. But when she asked Tuan to collect more of the cooling moss, she went out with him, leaving Maude with her brother.

Tuan looked at her. 'He's very bad, isn't he?'

Cliar nodded. 'Very. And even if he gets through tonight, he may be so ill I don't know if we'll be able to travel with him.'

'But we can't wait here for the Foxfaces to find us. And we have nothing to eat here, either. We just can't stay. We have to go on.'

Meanwhile, Maude was bathing her brother's face, which was dry as a dead leaf, not caring that there were tears streaming down her face. She was feeling so bad about every nasty thing she had ever said to Matthieu.

'If you get better, I swear I will never be mean to you

again,' she whispered, and to her amazement she heard a faint chuckle coming from her brother.

'I don't believe you at all,' he croaked. Then, still holding her hand, he sank into sleep.

When Cliar came back and felt his forehead, she smiled. 'The fever has broken, he's sleeping normally. Let's take turns to keep watch on him so that we all can have some sleep.'

'No, no, I'll mind him, he's my brother,' said Maude.

Tuan sighed. 'Come on, Maude, we don't need you getting tired and sick as well. Let us help you. I'll take the first shift and I promise I'll wake you if he gets worse.'

Maude suddenly remembered Dame Anna's words: she should not be too proud to ask for help when she needed it. She nodded reluctantly and forced the words out. 'You're right. Thank you. I thank you both.'

None of them had very much rest that night, between taking turns to watch over Matthieu and the fear of Foxface and his gang. Gile was no better than the children, restless and starting at every rustle in the undergrowth, every call of beast or bird. How different it was, thought Tuan, from the night they had spent out in the forest at Bunratty. That had been an adventure. They had had beds to go home to, a safe place to stay. Here, they had no idea where they were or how to find their way to safety.

CHAPTER 16

The Hermit in the Forest

he sun came up, the sky was clear and the air was warm. Matthieu was weak and shaky, but the fever was gone. He insisted that he could walk. For breakfast they had water and a few withered hazelnuts that Tuan had found on the floor of the forest. They would have to find the river and fish, or find some other source of food if they were going to eat at all today. But the good weather and the beauty of the forest in the early sunshine somehow cheered them up. Everything seemed to be coming alive – the small birds and forest animals, hares and deer and foxes that they glimpsed as they headed slowly into the light of the sunrise. Gile chased a rabbit around frantically, but being Gile, didn't manage to catch it.

If I had some wire I could trap a rabbit, thought Tuan, or

snare a fish. But all they had was the big knife they had taken from Ru, a stained and ugly weapon. Tuan carried it. Cliar refused to touch it; she said she could feel the horrible things that had been done with it. They stood in the dappled sunlight and looked at the thickets and briars and small trees that surrounded them on every side. There was no sign of the river that would have led them to Knockainy.

'Let's head for the west. We went east from the river when the gang captured us, so the river should be somewhere in this direction.' Tuan waited for Maude to contradict him; there was no guarantee that the river was to the west, for it could have coiled around on its course. But she said nothing. So Tuan led the way, hoping his guess had been right.

It was slow going. Tuan supported Matthieu on one side with Maude on the other, for he was so weak he could not walk on his own. The forest seemed to be becoming more rather than less dense, and Tuan had become less and less sure of the way. They reached a point where it seemed what might have been a path led eastwards, and Tuan was just about to lead the others that way when Cliar put her hand on his shoulder.

'Not that way,' she said.

'Why not?' asked Tuan.

'Look!' Cliar's voice was very excited, but when Tuan peered into the darkness to the west he could see nothing but the tangle of branches and leaves.

'Look again,' said Cliar, and Tuan heard Matthieu draw a sharp breath beside him. So he looked again and thought he saw a faint, silvery brightness in the leaves. He could not have said for sure it was the stag, but he could see by Cliar and Matthieu's eyes that they were certain that it was he.

'Very well, we'll go this way,' he said. And within minutes they noticed the light was getting stronger and they found themselves in a clearing. In the centre was a small hut, with smoke coming from the chimney and a white goat peacefully grazing in front of the door. A large black cat was sunning itself on the thatched roof, and Gile immediately made for it, barking his head off. Maude's frantic efforts to call him back made no difference; he barked and whined, scrabbling at the walls. The cat, however, seemed unworried, and began to wash himself.

A figure appeared in the doorway, dressed in a simple brown robe. It was an old man – a monk – with white hair and a long beard, and as soon as the children looked into his eyes they knew they had nothing to fear from him.

'Welcome,' he said. 'I hoped you would come this way. You must be hungry for breakfast.'

'But how did you know we might be coming?' said Maude.

'Oh, I have my scouts in the forest. They told me that you were close by.' Here he winked at a blackbird that had landed on his shoulder and was pecking affectionately at what remained of the monk's hair.

'My friend Dame Anna sent me a message asking me to look out for you this week back. Though she and I have our differences, we respect each other and know that we both will always try to work for the good.'

'But who are you?' asked Maude.

The old man smiled. 'It is a long time since I have bothered having a name. They called me Brother Angus once, when I was with my brothers in the abbey, but that is a long time ago. Most people just call me "the hermit in the wood", and that is what I am happiest to be known as, for there have been hermits here before me and I hope there will be others here long after me.'

'But do the gangs like Foxface's not attack you?' Maude persisted.

Tuan was shifting from foot to foot – there was a smell of

something delicious coming from the hut and he couldn't believe Maude was delaying them with her questions.

The hermit caught his eye. He smiled and said: 'Young Matthieu needs to be seated and to eat something quickly. Come in and eat with me and I will explain what I can.'

Over a delicious breakfast of duck eggs and mushrooms, the children told the hermit of their adventures and the hermit talked to them about the forest.

'There are two ways you can live in the forest. I live at peace with the woods and the wild things – and the woods and the wild things protect me. Foxface and his sort treat the forest as an enemy: they have gone wild in it. They care about nothing but where to find the next meal and how to keep warm in winter. But they are also deeply frightened of anything they do not understand. I have a few tricks up my sleeve to keep them away from my clearing, and to keep my goat, Socrates, and my ducks safe. Mist is useful, and the darkness that comes from nowhere, even in the middle of the day. You will be safe with me, though we must get you out of the forest soon. But rest a little first; you are all tired and Matthieu here needs some attention if he is to be able to continue on the journey. Unless he wishes to stay here with me?'

Matthieu thought for a moment. It was safe here, and the hermit was very kind. No more danger, no more discomfort for a while. It was tempting. But then Maude and Tuan and Cliar would go on without him. He decided he would rather go with his friends and see what adventures were waiting for them all.

He shook his head. 'Thank you, but I'll keep going.'

The hermit smiled. 'Very well. There will be a moon tonight and I think that would be a good time to continue back to the river and then southwards. The Maigue is not far from here.'

'Can you tell us the way to Knockainy?' asked Tuan, relieved at the thought that he would not have to try to remember the route.

The hermit shook his head. 'I have not been out of these woods these twenty years, and I came here from the west – I'm afraid I know nothing of the land east of the Maigue.'

Maude almost protested that they should get going immediately. Then she remembered her father's advice about campaigns: you cannot keep going on without rest, he'd often said, and it's important to pace your march. And Matthieu looked half-dead on his feet. She nodded, accepting the hermit's advice.

The others were more than happy to do as he had suggested, and during their day in the clearing they were introduced to Socrates the goat, Plato the cat, and the duck colony – who were called after the Nine Muses, but whose names the children found unpronounceable; they lived in the small stream that ran through the clearing.

'I think I would like a hermit's life,' said Matthieu drowsily, as they lay in the sun with their toes in the water of the stream.

'I would hate it,' said Maude. 'How boring it would be, nobody around and nothing happening.'

'But didn't you ever notice,' said Cliar, 'how you start to notice things when there are no people around? I used to see it on my trips to the forest, the further I went in, the quieter I felt inside myself and the more I saw.'

'I think I agree with Maude,' said Tuan. 'I like things happening around me. And I like people around me too. Even when they are annoying.' He grinned at Maude, who crossed her eyes and stuck her tongue out at him.

But then the hermit was calling them back to the hut and loading them with food. He began to give them directions.

'The moon is very bright tonight, which will help you on

your way,' he said. 'You must continue to follow the course of the river,' he said.

'At times it will be hard and you may have to walk through the river itself, as the undergrowth will be too thick on either side. And once you leave the forest, there will be marshes as well. Be very careful; it is easy to get stuck in the mud in some places. Outlaw is still at the priory at Knockainy, I'm sure, though my friends, the birds, do not go that far. When you see him you must tell him the hermit of the wood sends his greetings, and wishes to know when he will leave his life of action to pray with him a while.' He smiled, a little grimly. 'Though with the state of things in Thomond, I doubt if I will see him for some time.'

'My blessings on you, my children,' he said finally. 'God go with you.'

After his rest, and due to potions the hermit had given him, Matthieu was almost back to normal. He cast a rather wistful look behind him as they left the clearing, and Maude, trying to cheer him up, suggested that they sing. Maude was blissfully unaware of the fact that she could not sing a note; she only knew that when she and Matthieu sang together, he usually ended up in tears of laughter. After several minutes of listening to Maude's voice at its finest, Tuan suggested that perhaps Cliar might take a turn.

She shrugged. 'I don't know any songs – nobody ever sang to me.'

'Oh, you must know some.' He looked at her imploringly, but she shook her head.

'Very well, then, I'll sing,' said Tuan. He started one of the laments that his people sang at the loss of comrades in battle. It was a beautiful song, but very sad. As he sang, he suddenly became aware that Cliar had joined in with him, her sweet high treble blending with his. The tune she sang was the harmony of the melody he was singing, the part normally sung by the women of the Mac Conmara clan. The two of them sang on, and although Cliar sometimes faltered with the words, she continued confidently with the tune, right until the end of the song.

'Where did you learn that?' Tuan asked her, amazed. 'That song was never sung in Bunratty.'

Cliar shook her head, puzzled. 'I have no idea. It just came to me when I heard you singing.' She did not say that the song was somehow mixed up with her memories of the woman she dreamt of ... reaching her small hand into the woman's long red hair ...

Tuan shook his head, equally at a loss. 'That's the lament

of the Mac Conmara clan. Nobody but our people are supposed to know it. Perhaps you heard some of the hostages
sing it at Bunratty?'

Maude laughed. 'You're too fond of claiming everything
for the Mac Conmaras, Tuan! Music belongs to those who
sing it and listen to it with pleasure!'

Cliar said nothing. She knew that her memory of the song
went back much further than the time she had come to
Bunratty.

But now Matthieu interrupted. 'Look, it's the river.'

CHAPTER 17

KNOCKAINY

As the hermit had said, the ground was very rough along the river bank. The children often had to take their shoes off and wade, waist deep in water, in order to follow the course of the river. As they went upstream and the river became narrower, there were times when the branches of the trees met in a tangle over their heads. They had to struggle to get through the thickets. It was a scratched and grumpy group who finally decided to stop for rest after several hours. They had left the forest behind them and reached a relatively clear stretch of meadow and pastureland. They flung down their packs and threw themselves on the grass just as the moon set over the dark shapes of the trees.

'I'm so tired!' said Matthieu. 'And I'm hungry and I want

to sleep somewhere where stones and twigs don't dig into my back. Where I don't have to look at black beetles crawling past my nose. In a real bed. With linen and blankets!'

'Oh, don't be such a baby,' said Maude, then stopped in horror as she remembered that only the night before she had sworn never to be mean to Matthieu again.

She turned and gave her brother a quick hug. 'I know. It's all a bit miserable. Look, let's eat some of the food the hermit gave us. There's bread and honey and boiled eggs and cheese.'

Tuan cast an eye on the river. 'If someone would make a fire, I think we might be able to have some fish as well, they were jumping all around us as we made our way through the river during that last bit.'

They feasted that morning, then slept until the sun was high in the sky.

The next part of the journey was hard for all of them. Cliar and Maude said nothing, but they knew that Tuan was not sure of the route, and as neither had been listening to Prior Outlaw when he gave the directions, they could not help. Matthieu was not too worried – he was used to trusting other people to lead him along. But he was more tired than he would admit after his bout of fever. And Tuan was very anxious, knowing that the others were depending on him to lead the way.

While they followed the course of the Maigue, they were at least certain of their route; but Tuan was not at all sure where they were supposed to turn off. He knew that the river they were to take was one that would flow into the Maigue from the east, but he could not remember its name, nor when they would come to it. The further they went, the more nervous he felt. Was he leading everyone too far? Were they going the wrong way? They passed Adare, with its new Augustinian abbey, and were waved at by two fishermen monks as they travelled along the riverbank. Tuan thought of asking them the way to Knockainy, but he was afraid they would be questioned about who they were and where they were going. At Croom, the new walls of the town shone in the sunlight and they were tempted to go to the market there, for Maude, who still had silver coins sewn into the hem of her cloak, wanted to buy food. But the sight of the FitzGerald castle and the thought of soldiers decided them against stopping and in the end they crept under the bridge and past the town in darkness.

Then, one misty afternoon, while they tramped through the river rushes, damp and tired, they came to the mouth of a small river that flowed into the Maigue. They stopped, and Tuan looked at his companions.

'Do you think this is the river Outlaw talked about?' he asked.

Cliar shrugged. 'I'm afraid I wasn't really listening very hard that day.' Maude and Matthieu could not remember either, and Tuan felt desperate. Outlaw had entrusted the directions to him. And he had forgotten them.

He looked upriver.

'You really can't remember, can you?' said Cliar.

Tuan shook his head. No matter how hard he searched in his memory he couldn't get back to the place where Outlaw had told him the way to the Hospital at Knockainy.

'Do you think we should wait for the stag?' said Tuan. 'It was him, wasn't it, that led us towards the hermit's hut?'

Maude said in a slightly disgruntled tone, 'Well, I didn't see anything at all in the forest.'

But Cliar said: 'I'm not sure he just turns up on demand, Tuan. But I have another idea. Dame Anna showed me something once: it was a way to remember things you have forgotten. You go back to the time in your mind, and it's as if you were there again, so you know what was said. Do you want me to try it?'

'Is it witchcraft?' asked Tuan. Sometimes he wondered about Cliar. She really did have some very strange talents.

Cliar shook her head. 'No, I promise you it is not. It's just a different way of using your mind. Sit down, Tuan, and we'll try it. Maude and Matthieu, you must stay very quiet and still, and keep Gile from disturbing us.'

They settled themselves on a pile of rocks beside the little river, and Cliar sat opposite Tuan, looking into his eyes. She spoke quietly, in Irish, and within minutes Tuan felt himself relax, almost as if he were going to sleep, though not quite. It *is* magic, thought Matthieu, stroking Gile to keep him quiet. He exchanged glances with Maude. As they looked on, Tuan began to talk, in Irish too. Maude and Matthieu could recognise the words Outlaw and Knockainy, and then there was another word mentioned – Morningstar. Once again they looked at each other, for now they both remembered that that was the name of the river Outlaw had spoken about.

Finally, Cliar said something and Tuan opened his eyes, shaking his head to clear it.

'Did it work? Did I tell you what Outlaw told me?' he asked.

Cliar was grinning. 'Yes. He said that the river to take

was the Morningstar, not the Camog, which would be the first river we come to. This must be the Camog, for its name means "crooked river", and that's just what it looks like. We have to go on a bit farther before we turn off.'

So they passed the Camog, and finally came to where the Morningstar branched off to the east.

And this time all of them saw it. The Silver Stag stood in the sunlight where the Morningstar met the Maigue, his head bent, his front hoof scratching the ground in approval. And they knew the path they were taking was the right one. In a moment he was gone, but the children had been given fresh heart and courage.

✳ ✳ ✳

And they badly needed both. The river was small and shallow, so even if they had managed to keep the boat, they could not have used it here. It was hard to make their way along its winding and rocky course. But eventually they could see where the hills of Lough Gur rose to the north of the river. They left the river behind, finding a track that seemed to lead eastwards towards Knockainy. There were some houses along the way, but they saw nobody, except a guard dog who gave a desultory bark at Gile, and then went back to sleep, having obviously decided that the strange little group was no threat to him or his master.

By the end of the next day, which had been as warm and sunny as the one before, they had passed by the Hill of Knockainy. The hill was covered in yellow gorse, and cows and white horses grazed peacefully on its sides. As night fell, they could see the tower of the Hospitallers' church in the distance.

'Should we keep going?' said Tuan. 'If we arrive at night we will disturb everybody.'

'I think we need to talk to Outlaw as soon as we can,' said Maude. 'And surely he will feed us and give us a bed. And imagine not having to sleep on the ground … Let's keep going.'

The moon, now in its final crescent, was high in the sky when they reached the priory. Tall grey walls and iron gates rose before them, locked tight against the threat of outsiders. Dogs began to bark as they rang the bell, a loud peal which cut through the silence of the night like a knife. Within a few moments, a cowled figure came to the gate and enquired in a grumpy voice who the devil they were and what they thought they were doing arriving at a holy house at this unholy hour of the night.

Maude spoke in her most polite voice, curtsying. 'We do

apologise for our late arrival, but we are here to see Prior
Outlaw with a very important message. I am Lady Maude
and this is–'

The gatekeeper did not let her finish. 'I don't care who ye
are,' he said rudely. 'I can see ye're four scruffy children
and a mongrel dog. Bringing an important message? Is it
from the King ye're from?' He snorted with laughter. 'I'd
say not. I'd say all ye're bringing are empty bellies and begging ways. Maybe even thieving ways. And fleas.' He
looked meaningfully at Gile, who had chosen this moment
to scratch himself furiously.

'I do know one thing,' he continued, 'and that is that I am
not going to disturb the good Prior from his badly needed
slumbers for some gang of rapscallions. Be off, and come
back in the morning of ye must, but not before we have said
our office in the church and eaten. Though ye won't find
Prior Roger here then. He's to take the road to Dysert
O'Dea at first light.'

Cliar drew a breath and spoke with a hint of tears in her
voice. She could not believe they could have come so far
just to be turned away. 'Please, it's really important.'

The gatekeeper turned his back on them. Tuan thought of
something.

'Dame Anna of Bunratty sent us,' he said.

The gatekeeper turned, his face changed. 'Why the divil didn't you say that before now? Come in, come to the hall and I'll call the Prior immediately.'

The little monk unlatched the gate and they followed him across a courtyard through a doorway which led into a large hall. Like the Great Hall in Bunratty it was filled with long trestles and had a table across the top, close to the fireplace, which nearly filled one wall. They was a boy sleeping in front of the dying fire, and the monk who had let them in said testily, 'James, throw some wood on the fire and light the rushlights, the Prior will be coming down in a minute.'

He cast a glance at the children and added: 'And you had better bring some bread and milk from the kitchen for our visitors, and put down some pallets and blankets in the guest dormitory. They'll need water to wash too, or no doubt they'll be spreading wildlife amongst us, so they will. Hurry now,' he added, as the boy stood before him, still half-asleep. 'Sooner started, sooner finished.' The lad scuttled away, the monk following him, muttering under his breath.

The children stood in front of the fire, warming themselves. What they wanted most of all, even more than food, was to lie down and sleep, safe in the knowledge that there were no dangers around them.

How strange, thought Tuan. For the first time in my life I really appreciate stone walls and enclosed rooms.

A moment later Outlaw appeared, looking as if he had not been asleep at all.

'Welcome, my children,' he said, 'Sit down and take some wine to warm yourselves up – I have told James to get you some hot broth and meat. You look as if you are in need of care. God knows how you got here through such wild countryside. You must tell me all your adventures. How Dame Anna could have sent you out like this into the wilderness on your own I do not know.'

Cliar shifted uneasily. She decided to tell the truth.

'Sir, she did not exactly send us out; but she needed to get a message to you and we ... we needed to leave Bunratty.'

'We will talk of that later. What was the message?'

'She and I saw something in the flames of her fire – a terrible defeat for the English at Dysert O'Dea. I saw Sir Richard wounded. She wanted to tell you not to join them there, that defeat was inevitable. That there would be terrible loss of life.'

Prior Roger gave a long sigh. 'So, I am not to go to Dysert

O'Dea? It looks bad for the English, then, if she has already seen Sir Richard's death. I have heard rumours of treachery against Sir Richard, but hoped that they were false ...'

He sighed again and looked deep into the fire for a few minutes, as if by looking into the flames he could find an answer – as if, like Dame Anna, he could see the future there. But it seemed he saw nothing, for after a few moments he shook his head impatiently. Then he began talking quietly to himself.

'So what should I do? Stay here or head to the north, where the Scots are creating havoc? Or go to Bunratty and try to keep the peace there and in the south? I must think. But first, children, you must eat and drink and then go to bed. You look dead on your feet. We will talk more in the morning.'

CHAPTER 18

Dysert O'Dea

he children slept until well after dawn, and it was only when James entered their room with warm water for washing that they woke up. He had found clothing for them all, though all he had managed to find for Cliar and Maude were boy's trousers and jerkins. But they did not care. They were just very glad not to have to wear the ragged and filthy clothes they had been wearing for many days. They ate in the dormitory and then they were brought to the Great Hall, where Prior Roger was engaged in what seemed to be a kind of conference with some of the other brothers. He smiled at them as they entered the room.

'Well, children, you have done us a great service with your message. I thank you for that. But I must ask what you will do now? I plan to return to Bunratty, to aid the Lady

Johanna if possible, and I will take you all with me, if that is what you wish.'

The children exchanged glances. They had been so intent on carrying out their mission they had not thought beyond it.

Tuan spoke first. 'Sir, it would be a point of honour for me to return to Bunratty, but I fear the Lady Johanna plans to have me harmed – indeed killed. Maude heard her making plans for my death with Sir Richard. They have broken their promise, so the agreement binds me no more. I am free to go back to my own people. But I don't know if I can reach my home, for I have no boat and my people's lands are very far away from here.'

Outlaw frowned. 'That was not well done of Sir Richard and the Lady Johanna. But I will stand surety for you now. I will not let any harm come to you,' said Outlaw. 'And we shall try to get you back to your own people as soon as we can, for the time for hostages is over. Come with me first to Bunratty, and I will make sure that you reach the lands beyond Cratloe safely.' He turned to Cliar. 'And you, Cliar, what do you wish to do?'

She sighed. 'I'll go back to Bunratty, I suppose, and continue to work in the kitchen. I have nowhere else to go. And

I want to make sure that Dame Anna is safe. She was sleeping so strangely the last time I saw her.'

'Do not be concerned for Dame Anna, child. She disappears at times, like the sun or the moon, but she always—returns. And, Cliar, it may be that you have more choices than you think you have,' said Outlaw. 'But it would be as well for you to return to the castle for the present. As it is for you two – no, Maude, do not protest – I promise you that you will not be long in Bunratty. I may have news for you soon, but I will say nothing now for fear of disappointing you. For the present, I want the two of you close by my side. Will you trust me to do what is best for you?'

Could they? thought Maude. Could they trust this man, famous for his cleverness and word-craft? But they really had no choice. And her father had trusted the Hospitallers. That would have to be enough. She nodded.

'Good, then. We ride out tomorrow. Today you must rest, for it will be a long journey, though this time you will not have to go on foot. Tuan and Maude, perhaps you could go and talk to Brother Arthur, the groom? You can help him choose which horses you will each ride.' A tall brother with a weathered face stepped forward, smiling.

'And you, Cliar,' he nodded towards a short, fat brother,

'Brother Brian will take you to the infirmary, where he will talk to you about the ways of healing we use here. This place is known as Hospital for good reasons. I know that will interest you. Matthieu, you may go to the scriptorium with Brother Hugh; he has many manuscripts to show you, that I think you will like to see.'

Next morning they set out on the way back to Bunratty. It was a very different journey from the one they had made to Knockainy. As Outlaw had said, long days were spent in the saddle, but they felt safe and protected by Outlaw and his soldier monks. And the weather was beautiful. They rode in sunshine through green pastures flecked with cowslips and buttercups, by ditches where young ferns were uncurling into the light. Everywhere they stopped, they were welcomed, for Outlaw was known and respected throughout this part of the world.

While they rode, Outlaw asked them to tell him of their adventures on their way to him. He, in turn, told them tales of his campaigns, of his journeys far into the wild worlds of lake and mountain and forest to the north and west, where one could travel for days and not meet a human soul. He also told them about the city of Dublin, with its castle and great walls, and about the Hospitaller's house in Kilmainham, one of the most important priories in Ireland. The days went quickly, almost too quickly, for none of them quite knew what to expect when they reached Bunratty.

Tuan was anxious lest he would somehow be prevented from continuing his journey back to his parents. To Maude and Matthieu, Bunratty had become a prison and they were horrified at the thought of a life spent there with Lady Johanna, who would surely give them no freedom at all after their escape. Maude was especially fearful, in case Lady Johanna would go ahead with the plan to marry her off to the young De Burgh. Cliar was also very unhappy at the thought of returning to Bunratty. But she knew she had to go back. She had to be sure that Dame Anna had woken from that strange sleep, and that all was well with her.

Just after sunrise one morning, after a night when the moon gleamed fiercely against a sky awash with bright stars, Tuan woke and went to join the sentry, Brother Arthur, who was guarding the camp.

'Look there,' Brother Arthur said, 'can you see something coming over that ridge to the north?'

Tuan looked hard and saw something moving. Within minutes it became the shape of a horseman, racing his horse over the green hill which had sheltered them from the western wind.

'He's certainly in a hurry,' said Brother Arthur. 'You run and get the Prior, lad. I'll keep an eye here to make sure it's a friend.' A few moments later, he squinted. 'Well, if it isn't one of Sir Richard's troops. I recognise the livery.'

The horseman arrived, breathless and red-faced. He threw himself from his horse to bow to Prior Roger. The children recognised him as Henry, one of the guardsmen of the castle. His eyes were wild and his armour gone, his clothes were tattered and blood-stained.

'My Lord, I have terrible news for you. Sir Richard has been killed at Dysert O'Dea. His forces are scattered. Many are dead or taken prisoner by the Irish.'

Prior Roger took the man by the arm. 'Here, friend, seat yourself.' He turned to one of the servants. 'Bring drink and food quickly, and look to the horse. Now, my brother, tell me what you can.'

The children stood silently while the man told his story. Even though they had known that Sir Richard would be killed in the battle, it was still a shock to hear that it had actually happened. Sir Richard De Clare, the proud Lord of Bunratty, the great warrior, was no more.

'It was terrible to see. We went bravely to the battle at Dysert; our spirits were high, for our spies had told us that we far outnumbered the Irish.' Henry spat. 'There was some treachery there. And Fat John was a part of it.'

'We came across the river,' he continued, 'and there was an old woman there, washing clothes, and she looked at Sir Richard and said: "*You will not return from this battle. Red will be your fine white flesh and red will be the white towers of your fine castle.*" And then we saw the water was turned red, and the shirt she was washing was covered in blood. And Sir Richard became angry and raised his sword, but when we looked again the dame was gone, and there was nothing but a heron watching us, with a bright, knowing eye. And they say that the banshees to the east set up a terrible wailing that night, for though An Claraghmore was Norman English, he was also a great warrior and lord of his people.'

The man paused and took a deep breath.

'So we came into the valley. Everything was green but the land was silent, strangely silent, as if the birds of the air had deserted the place. And we thought that the Irish had fled away for fear of us. We pitched camp at the place called Ruan. Its name might well have been Ruin, that place! The next morning Sir Richard divided us into three parts, sending some of us to harry the O'Dea cattle and take on the forces in the woods to the west. Sir Richard himself led the attack on a small force that came to meet us at the ford of the river. We rode towards them so proudly ...'

The man paused and swallowed.

'There were so few of them it seemed as if we should be able to defeat them easily, but it was a trap. They drew us across the ford, and then ... then hundreds more rose up, as if from the very earth, and attacked us. There was a great rushing and howling as they sang out their accursed war cries and they came upon us from all sides. We had no hope of defeating them. The blood was everywhere, staining the river red. I saw Sir Richard killed, with a blow from behind from an axe. It split his helmet and his mail and he fell to the ground, one of his feet still caught in his stirrups. His horse panicked, and ran with him, caught like that for some way, until his page came and released his foot. Then his horse fell too, hit by an arrow, shrieking like a man in his agony. And after that there was slaughter and more slaughter. I never wish to see such slaughter again.' The man stopped, exhausted.

'But how did the Irish know that Sir Richard was going to

attack Dysert O'Dea?' asked Prior Roger.

'There were spies in his own army, sending scouts to the clans. They say Fat John was the main one, and that was why he did not ride with Sir Richard. They say he was paid well, but little good the gold has done him. One of Sir Richard's loyal men – Robert the Marshal – took his revenge on him, for he lives no more. He was found with his face down in the Shannon, drowned.'

The children exchanged glances. At least there was one less horror in their world.

Tuan did not know what to feel. Should he be glad that the English had been defeated? Of course he was; yet it all seemed so sad and horrible; such a waste of men's lives. He could see it, the battlefield, hear the cries of men and horses, and feel the pain and fear everywhere around him. It was such a terrible story for such a beautiful morning.

'De Clare then is dead, then, and the castle undefended,' said Prior Roger, his face grim. 'The word will soon spread that Bunratty is no longer protected. We must go as quickly as we can to Lady Johanna and the child. We'll cross the Shannon at Limerick.'

They rode as fast as they could into the lowlands by the Shannon, and arrived at the gates of Limerick just before

they were due to be closed for the night. The sentries recognised Outlaw and asked him if he was going to King John's
castle, but he shook his head.

'We ride as early as we can in the morning; I will stay in
the inn that the brothers use here. I am on private business,
on my way to Bunratty.'

As they made their way in the twilight through the
narrow streets, noisy and crowded and smelling strongly
of horse manure and human sweat, Tuan and Cliar kept
close to Prior Outlaw. Neither had been in a town before,
and they were slightly awed by the sight of so many
people, and so many buildings all cramped in together, but
Maude and Matthieu told them that it was a very small
town by comparison to the ones they had seen – Rome and
Paris and Antwerp.

Outlaw laughed. 'You must come to Dublin,' he told
Tuan and Cliar, 'for it is bigger and has its castles and
towers and cathedrals. And as I have told you, our house at
Kilmainham is a goodly one.'

They were soon at the inn, a low, thatched building, its
courtyard protected from the street by a grey stone wall. A
wooden door was the only entry and it was closed tight.
Cliar knew she would like the place as soon as she saw that

the sign hanging outside showed a magnificent stag standing proudly against the background of a green forest.
Outlaw knocked twice and the innkeeper, a tall, stout man
with a merry face, opened up and greeted them. After
instructing the grooms to look after the horses, he shook
Prior Outlaw's hand and said: 'Welcome to the Stag's
Head. 'Tis a pity I did not know you were coming, for I have
already given my best room to a knight that came here with
some of your brothers just yesterday. A fine man he is, and
it seems that he's on his way to Bunratty too.'

He turned as a tall, fair-haired man came out the door of
the inn. He was so tall he had to stoop to come through.

'Ah, Sir Baldwin!' the innkeeper said, 'I was just telling
these good folk my best room is ...'

But the fair-haired knight was not paying any attention to
the landlord. Nor was anyone else, for with squeals of joy
Matthieu and Maude had run towards him, and the knight
had gathered them both up in his arms.

'Well, this is a surprise, but a good one,' said Outlaw.
'Sir Baldwin, I thought you would stay in Kilmainham until
I brought your children to you.'

Maude turned to Outlaw. 'You knew it – you knew our
father was alive and did not tell us?'

'Do not be angry, child. I could not be totally sure it was your father, and I did not want to raise false hopes. I had word from Dublin that a knight was lately returned from the lands to the east, a knight who had come to Ireland to search for his children. He had been told that the boy and girl had been brought to Ireland, but by some confusion thought them in Dublin rather than here in Bunratty. I sent a message that he should wait in Kilmainham until I could bring you there in safety.'

The fair man, his arms still around Maude and Matthieu, smiled. 'How could I stay away when I knew them to be here? And after so long an absence! I tell you, it is not such a long journey when you travel with friends. We have heard strange stories along the way, Outlaw, of four children travelling through the wilderness and of strange doings in the castle.'

'We will tell you everything. You should be proud of your children's courage and hardiness. And they have found good friends – this is Tuan, of the Mac Conmaras, and the Lady Cliar, the apprentice of Dame Anna.'

The knight did his best to bow to Tuan and Cliar. It was hard for him to do so, with Maude and Matthieu still clinging to him on either side. Maude was crying, not caring that everyone could see that there were tears streaming down her face. Her father took out his kerchief and wiped her eyes.

'There, sweetheart, cry no more. For I am determined I will not let you two out of my care again. If I had not been wounded and left to rot in a stinking prison I would have been back to you long before now. It was the thought of seeing you two that kept me alive, and kept me going on the long road back to England. I could not believe it when I reached Dorset and found that you were no longer there.'

Cliar looked closely at Sir Baldwin. It seemed that even he was having difficulty keeping the tears out of his eyes.

It was a wonderful evening. Sir Baldwin told them stories of his capture and eventual escape from his captors. Maude and Matthieu, constantly interrupting and contradicting each other as to what had actually happened, told their father of their adventures since he had seen them last. They talked late into the night, and it was Prior Roger who finally said they should get some rest, for they were to rise before dawn the following day, in order to reach Bunratty early.

The route to Bunratty led them along the curve of the Shannon, and they travelled with the rising sun at their backs. As they rounded a bend in the river, they saw a light in the sky ahead of them, almost as if another sun was rising to the west. Prior Outlaw pulled up, his eyes screwed up in order to see into the distance.

'God help us, it looks as if we are too late. That light is flame, and the smoke in the distance must be the castle. The Irish have already set it burning.' He broke into a gallop.

CHAPTER 19

Red and White and
Black Shall Be

 s they came closer to Bunratty, they could see that the white tower of the castle was wrapped in red flames. Black smoke rose from it, dark against the green sea of grass and trees. Cliar thought of Dame Anna's words: *Red and white and black shall be Bunratty*, and shivered.

The village too was on fire, and as they came near to it, they could see the villagers running about, carrying bales of hay and herding animals away from the flames. Yet everyone seemed to have an air of purpose rather than panic about them. One or two people even smiled and waved at their little group. Then they realised that most of the activity seemed to be centred on moving bundles down to the bank of the Shannon, where a tall ship was docked. There was no sign of any Irish attackers.

Prior Outlaw pulled up his horse.

'I cannot credit it,' he said, shaking his head in disbelief. 'I cannot believe even she would do it.'

'What do you mean?' asked Tuan.

'Let us find the mistress of the castle as quickly as we can. Here,' he called to a villager who was passing with a load of grain on his back, 'can you tell me where the Lady Johanna is?'

'Why, down in the ship, counting out what is being loaded, of course. Lord, she has us all scarified. A tough taskmaster, I'll tell you, she is. Tougher yet than any man, even Sir Richard, God bless his poor soul.'

They made their way to the dock, and there was Lady Johanna in the forecastle, a list in her hand, marking off the goods as they were loaded on board.

Prior Roger dismounted and bowed to her from the shore.

'I mourn your loss with you, my lady,' were his first words. 'Sir Richard was a great warrior.'

Lady Johanna looked at him, her eyes bleak as the coldest of winters. She raised her pale eyebrows.

'Myself, I have no time to mourn,' she declared. 'I must be busy with this task. If you wish to stay with me and help, you are welcome. If you wish to hinder me, I bid you begone.'

Prior Roger asked quietly, 'What has happened to the castle, lady? Who set it afire?'

Lady Johanna's lip curled. 'Who set it afire? I did. I have burnt it and the village so they may not fall into the hands of the Irish. And I am glad to see it destroyed, cleared forever from the face of the earth, for home it never was to me. And now I am taking my goods away from this devilish place. I will sail up the Shannon to Limerick. From thence I will take a ship to my father's lands in England. My child will be safe there and grow up in a civilised place. Never again will I set foot in this accursed country.'

Her sour expression was set like stone. That is a look, thought Cliar, that will never leave her face.

There was silence as the meaning of what Lady Johanna had said sank in. Then she spoke again.

'I see you have my wards with you. My disobedient wards. But I suppose it is my duty to take them back to England with me, though they will be of no use to me. Just two more mouths to feed! Let us hope I can find some sort of useful work for them … Maude, Matthieu, come on board. Maude, you must get changed out of that outrageous outfit, at once.'

The children looked at their father, thinking of how it might have been if he had not come for them.

'Hurry now,' Lady Johanna said impatiently. She peered at Cliar. 'Humph! I see you have my runaway Irish servant with you too. I have no use for her – if she showed such disobedience once, it could happen again. She may do as she wishes. I will not feed her.'

'My lady,' said Cliar, 'where is Margaret? And Dame Anna?'

'Oh, Margaret went to her son's farm after you disappeared. Such impudence I had from her, when I told her we were going back to England. She has no desire to leave Bunratty, she said, for her home is here. Home indeed! She will, no doubt, end up being burned in her bed by the Irish. But it was as well, for I have not room for every villager. How they will make do in this land now I do not know. Or care.' She turned her attention to the dogs that were being driven onto the ship, whining and barking in protest. 'There now, down in the hold with them, hurry them up …'

The little group gazed at the burning white towers. The

smell of the fire was sharp in their nostrils. How strange, thought Cliar, that someone would rather see a whole world go up in smoke than leave it for another to conquer.

Then, as they watched, a flock of white pigeons flew from the north west tower.

At the very moment Maude asked, 'But where is Dame Anna?'

Lady Johanna shrugged. 'She refused to leave her tower when I sent word of my plans. There was nothing I could do. I thought she would move fast enough when the flames started licking at her heels, but it seems that she is even more stubborn than I thought. Hurry, girl, and get yourself on board. You can help arrange the smaller boxes in the hold, and you too, Matthieu, make haste.'

But now Sir Baldwin spoke. 'Lady Johanna, I am the children's father. I thank you for your' – he paused for a moment, as if deciding what word to use – 'for your care of them. But now they are with me and I will keep them close.'

Lady Johanna threw her hands up. 'Well, if that is the case, take them with you and welcome! I never could learn to love either of them and their strange eastern ways. Now, I have no time for this prattle. Heigh ho!' she shrieked at a villager who was trying to herd a pig up the gangway, 'I told you to wait and bring them all on together!' She grabbed the man's stick and began to hit him with it, and he rapidly got himself and his pig out of her range.

Cliar was tugging at Outlaw's sleeve. 'Prior Outlaw? Dame Anna! Please can we go to her tower? We must get her to come out. Look at the flames – they'll block the staircase soon.'

Outlaw nodded. 'Yes, let us go. Though I fear the fire has taken too strong a hold for us to help much.'

As the children made their way towards the tower, they were filled with a strange mix of emotions. What Maude felt was mostly joy; her father was alive and she was with him. Yet, though she had never loved Bunratty, it was sad to see the lovely towers burn. It had, after all, been a refuge of a sort to her and her brother. Matthieu was simply full of delight. He was with his father, and from now on he would be able to talk to him, really talk to him again, instead of imagining the conversations they might have together. That was all he wanted from life.

Tuan felt little except concern for Dame Anna. Bunratty had been a prison to him and nothing more. He was wondering if Prior Roger would go back to Hospital now. If he did, Tuan wondered how he would get back to his own people, through a land filled with English soldiers. A land where speaking with the wrong accent could leave you with your throat slit.

And Cliar was crying quietly. She was the only one who could see that the faint figures of the ghosts were leaving Bunratty, drifting up like plumes of smoke from the flames, fading into air and brightness. She felt happy for them, for she knew that the pain that had tied them to the castle was gone now. But they had been part of the castle and part of her life and now she would never see them again. Bunratty, despite everything, had been the only home she had ever known. What would she do now? Perhaps she could make her home with Margaret, in the village? But most of the village was burning, and how long could it last without the protection of the castle? And if she did spend the rest of her life there, she had a horrible feeling she knew what would happen. She would end up marrying Fred, Margaret's son. Fred was kind, like Margaret, but he was not at all interesting. She would spend her days listening to him talk about the weather and his four cows and his hayfield and his bunions. She would never learn the ways of healing that Dame Anna had promised to teach her. For how could Dame Anna have survived the fire?

When the little group made their way cautiously into the bailey they found that everyone else had left, for the fire was spreading quickly throughout the castle. The north west tower was a column of flame. Outlaw shook his head. There was no way they could go in. Strangely, though, the smoke that came from these flames was not the acrid, stinging smoke that came from the rest of the castle. It smelt sweet and strong, like hawthorn blossom. But they could not get close to the door, for the flames were hotter here than anywhere else. From the distance, though, they could see that the small, carved figure beside the door was black as night.

They stood, watching the tower burn.

'I'm sorry, children, there is nothing we can do,' said Outlaw. He led them across the drawbridge, away from the fire.

They stood in silence. Tears were streaming down Cliar's face.

Sir Baldwin whistled softly, watching the flames. 'It is a sad day to see such a great castle burn.'

It was Outlaw who answered. 'It is indeed, and by the hand of the lady of the castle. I cannot see Lady Johanna's children returning here. This is the end of the De Clares at Bunratty.'

Sir Baldwin nodded. 'The end of the De Clares, indeed. But no doubt the battles will continue over who owns this fair land.'

There was a great crackling noise. They all looked upwards; the roof of the north west tower splintered and caved in, falling downwards in a shower of fiery sparks.

Everyone thought of Dame Anna. The flames had spread everywhere; the drawbridge they had crossed over only a few minutes before was already on fire.

But now a figure was walking across the fiery bridge, out of the flame-filled castle gate. A figure dressed in a black cloak, a figure with white hair streaming around her. A figure followed by a flock of birds – ravens and pigeons and the small birds from the hedgerows. Flying above her head was a white owl and a black dove.

The woman's face was white as the owl's feathers and her eyes burned with a dark flame.

The group stared. Even Outlaw found nothing to say. There was something in this figure that made every one of them feel full of awe.

But now Dame Anna smiled. 'Once again, you have done well, children. And you will have your reward. Outlaw, we must talk, but not until you have done the business you need to do in the north.'

'But where will you go? What will happen to you?' asked Cliar. 'Bunratty is destroyed.'

Dame Anna smiled. 'Do not be concerned for me, child. I will always find a place of safety. But you, Cliar, what will *you* do now?'

Prior Outlaw replied. 'We must leave here, for I must return to Dublin. But on my way I will bring Tuan back to his people east of Cratloe. And Cliar may come with me to Kilmainham, if she so wishes.'

Maude said: 'But she must come with us! She's part of our family now!' Matthieu nodded in agreement.

Then Tuan broke in. 'No, she must come to my family. My parents will love her – she seems half a Mac Conmara already!'

Dame Anna smiled again. 'Well, child, it seems you have found a family, indeed more than one. But I have one more choice to give you. Would you like to come with me, deep into the mountains, and learn more of what I have taught you? Of healing plants and herbs, of the wisdom of the earth and the trees? Of how to read flame in the water and the messages sent by the flight of birds? If you agree, we will go into the hills together, and I will teach you all that I know.'

Cliar hesitated only a moment. She knew where her fate would lead. Perhaps she had known it from that first day, from that first step she had taken into Dame Anna's tower. She smiled at her companions.

'Thanks to you all,' she said. 'You can never know how grateful I am to be wanted, to be welcomed. And I hope we'll all meet again, often, for you are like my family to me now. But my home is with Dame Anna. I'll go with you, Dame Anna, and learn from you. And try to use what I have learned to help others.'

Dame Anna nodded. 'We will find a place until Bunratty castle rises again – for rise it will. Listen carefully, and I will tell you something of what I foresee. This stone and wood will change their form, like all things made by man. But something at the heart of this place will never pass away. The castle will rise again, though those that live in it may not be Norman or English. Cliar, you have already learned that we serve not lord nor chieftain, Norman nor English nor Irish, but only those who have need of our skill. Those people will live in the castle and in the little houses in the shelter of its walls, and we, and those healers who follow us, will care for them all. Bunratty will remain and there will always be a wise woman there, though she may wear a different face and speak a different tongue. And there will always be a Silver Stag in the woods around the castle, though few will see it, and fewer still believe what they have seen.'

There was silence, except for the soft crackling of the flames. Above them, the birds circled in the blue air.

※ ※ ※

Something else was moving out of the inferno, silver against the red and gold of the flames. It walked slowly through the fire, unharmed by it. It stood for a moment and looked towards them in all its pale, shining beauty, raising one delicate hoof as if in salutation. Then it moved away, running swiftly towards the south, where the Shannon flowed into the silvery vastness of the western sea.

HISTORICAL NOTE

Most of the characters in this book, including Tuan, Cliar, Maude and Matthieu, are fictional ones. Some, however, were real people, and many of the events described in the story actually happened in County Clare in May 1318.

BUNRATTY, of course, still exists, although the castle that one can see there nowadays was built in the second half of the fifteenth century. The original settlement at Bunratty was a Viking trading post dating from the end of the tenth century, and the first castle, a timber one, was built by the Norman knight Richard De Muscegros around 1250.

By 1277 Bunratty was in the hands of Thomas De Clare, and he constructed the first stone castle on the site. Bunratty was a thriving village by this time, and a regular fair was held there. Sir Thomas De Clare was a brave soldier, but was known for his treachery. He did indeed, kill Brian Rua while he was a guest under his roof, as in the story, and he also killed the two hostages mentioned as ghosts.

His son, Sir Richard De Clare, became Lord of Bunratty after his older brother Gilbert died. Richard De Clare was known as 'An Claraghmore'(the Great De Clare), for he was a great lord and soldier. He was killed at the battle of Dysert O'Dea in May 1318, and the Irish annals tell of the banshees wailing before his death and of his meeting with the washerwoman at the ford.

His wife Johanna, who was English by birth, left Bunratty as soon as the news of his death reached her. She burned the castle to the ground and set off for England, never to return. De Clare's heir died in England and the castle passed into the hands of his sisters, who took no interest in it.

Bunratty was let go to waste for years after the battle of Dysert O'Dea in 1318, and was completely destroyed by the O'Briens and the Mac Conmaras (McNamaras) in 1322. The Norman Thomas De Rokeby built a new castle on the site in 1355, but that too was destroyed two years later.

When the castle rose again it was as a Gaelic tower house, built by the Mac Conmaras during the second half of the fifteenth century. It was later taken and held by the O'Briens from the end of that century until the 1650s, when it was taken by Cromwell's army under General Ludlow. The Studdart family took possession of Bunratty and its lands from 1725 and lived in the castle until 1804, when they moved to the adjoining manor house. The castle was allowed to fall into ruin until purchased by Lord Gort in the 1950s. It has now been magnificently restored and is at the centre of a Folk Park owned by the state.

If you visit Bunratty today, look out for the door with the strange carving beside it and the great antlers decorating the walls of the Great Hall.

ROGER OUTLAW, Prior of the Knights Hospitallers in Ireland, is also an historical character. The Hospitallers were soldiers as well as monks and Outlaw was known as a skilful diplomat as well as being a great soldier. He held high office in Ireland throughout his career and the records state that he was often sent out to 'parley with the Irish'. When his cousin, Alice Kyteler, was accused of witchcraft,

Prior Roger was instrumental in saving her from death.

THE O'BRIENS were lords of the Gaelic tribes in Thomond and the Mac Conmaras were among their greatest supporters. There were constant battles between contenders for the lordship of the O'Brien clan and for control of the kingdom of Thomond. At the time of the story, there were two members of the clan competing for the lordship. Alliances between the Gaelic tribes and the Norman settlers shifted and changed all the time.

THOMOND, the ancient name for the area encompassing parts of Clare, Limerick and north Tipperary, was plagued by these ongoing battles. Matters were not helped by the terrible weather of the second decade of the fourteenth century, which resulted in famine throughout Europe.

HOSTAGES: Tuan's position as a hostage was not unusual at this period. Hostage taking, as a means of making sure that the enemy did not attack, was common in medieval Ireland, both between the Gaelic tribes and with the Normans.

By Eithne Massey

History, myth and legend collide in this thrilling novelisation of the full-length Oscar nominated animated feature *The Secret of Kells*.

For as long as he can remember, Brendan has never been allowed outside the monastery of Kells. Then, one day, the famous illuminator, Aidan of Iona, arrives with his cat, Pangur Bán, and everything changes. Brendan longs to help Aidan with the Great Book. Aidan needs special ink berries that can only be found in the forest. But Brendan's uncle, Abbot Cellach, forbids him to set foot outside the walls. 'The Northmen are coming,' he warns. 'We are all in danger!'

In the dark of the night, Brendan defies his uncle and sneaks into the forest. There he is attacked by wolves and meets a strange fairy girl. Together they find the berries, but they also make another terrifying discovery. They stumble on the cave of Crom Cruach, the Dark One …

Can Brendan outwit the serpent god? Will the walls of Kells protect Brendan and the monks from the invading Vikings? And will the Great Book ever be finished?

This novel brings to life the fictionalised story of Brendan, a young monk in the monastery of Kells and his part in the completion of one of the world's most famous and treasured books, The Book of Kells.

By Eithne Massey

Back home in Brazil, Roberto loved playing football. Now he lives in Ireland, and he'd really like to have a game with the boys in the park, but he's too shy.

When his granny reminds him of the Brazilian story of the dreaming tree, he doesn't see how a story can help him …

But maybe it can!

By Eithne Massey

For younger children, a fantastic collection of the great Irish legends.

Stories from long, long ago, part of an ancient oral tradition, handed down from generation to generation and written down by the Christian monks of medieval Ireland.

STORIES The Salmon of Knowledge, How Cú Chulainn Got His Name, The Children of Lir, The King with Donkey's Ears, Fionn and the Giant.

Coming soon from Eithne Massey

Where the Stones Sing

A vivid story of one girl's fight for survival
in darkest medieval Dublin
SET IN CHRIST CHURCH CATHEDRAL

As the spectre of the Black Death hovers over the city, Kate is living a lie, posing as a boy in the great Christ Church choir. She must keep her secret from everyone ... even her new friends Tom and Jack.

When Jack is cruelly taken by the plague, Kate turns to the mysterious voices in the church for comfort. But the cathedral is also home to powerful enemies who are determined to destroy the singer ... in the most terrible way imaginable.

Kate will need great strength, talent and help from unexpected quarters just to survive.

OTHER IRISH HISTORICAL NOVELS FROM THE O'BRIEN PRESS

EARLY IRELAND

GAELIC IRELAND

The tense story of tribal conflict in early Ireland. A boy, fostered with a remote tribe, becomes involved in a local feud, and with the fate of his belove Fran, the chieftain's daughter.

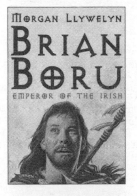

THE IRISH vs THE DANES *

A story set in ninth-century Ireland, when the Gaelic chieftains faught each other as well as the Danes. Tells the extraordinary tale, from childhood to death, of the great Brian Boru, King of Munster and High King, who faught and died at the Battle of Clontarf in 1014.

THE NORMAN PERIOD *

The story of the most famous Norman of them all: Strongbow, one of the first Normans to come to Ireland. He married Aoife, the daughter of the King of Leinster. The story is told alternately from both points of view, Aoife's and Strongbow's.

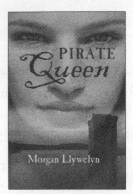

ELIZABETHAN IRELAND *

The story of a unique woman, Grace O'Malley (Granuaile), pirate and chieftain – a thorn in the side of the English and a particular scourge of Queen Elizabeth I. This is the amazing and exciting account of her wild adventures and great achievements.

ELIZABETHAN IRELAND *

The capture of Red Hugh O'Donnell and his harrowing escape through the snows from Dublin Castle into the Wicklow mountains, is a story that has intrigued people down through the centuries. Here it is told in all its detail, horror – and heroics.

THE FLIGHT OF THE EARLS *

After the Battle of Kinsale, there is very little left in Ireland for the Irish chieftains and their families. Here we encounter Hugh O'Neill, and read of the exciting chase for his young son, Con, whom he wishes to take with him to the Continent. But can Con be found in time?

THE FAMINE *

Eily, Michael and Peggy are left on their own during the Great Famine. They must search for their Great Aunts whom they have heard of only in their mother's stories. The children undertake a long journey full of danger and challenge.

EMIGRATION *

Peggy emigrates at the age of thirteen to look for a new life in America. We follow her sad departure, the treacherous boat journey, and her arrival in the New World. We read of her work as a maid in a big house, and her plans to go to the wild west.

THE LAND

Eily has stayed at home, married, and has her own little family. But they are in constant danger of being thrown off the patch of land that they must rent. How can they ever acquire a farm of their own? Is there any hope of a good future for Eily's children?

EARLY 20th CENTURY IRELAND

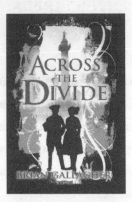

THE LOCKOUT 1913 *

Liam and Nora become friends at the Feis Ceoil, but their fathers are on opposite sides during the Dublin lockout. One is a striking worker, the other a wealthy employer. Can their friendship survive this divide?

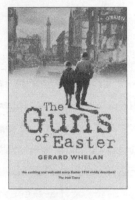

THE EASTER RISING 1916 *

Young Jimmy Conway observes the events of the Rising on his own doorstep where he lives in the nearby tenements. His father is away fighting at the Great War, and his uncle is with the rebels. But where does Jimmy stand?

THE EASTER RISING 1916 *

John Joe and Roger are pupils at Padraic Pearse's famous school, St Enda's. They hear about the Rising, but are too young to take part. However, they find their way into the city centre and become caught up in the dramatic events of the rebellion.

WOMEN'S SUFFRAGE *

Amelia is from a wealthy Quaker family. But when her mother is sent to prison for protest activities, Amelia must grow up fast and learn to care for the family. She also has to deal with her father's bankruptcy. Poor Amelia, the party girl! Will this make or break her?

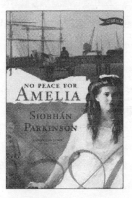

THE GREAT WAR *

Amelia, now sixteen, falls in love with Frederick. He is also a Quaker, and they are pacifists. But when Frederick volunteers to go to war, what should Amelia think? Then, there's the soldier that she and the servant girl hide in the garden. War is dangerous – at home and abroad.

WAR OF INDEPENDENCE *

There are hints of war all over Ireland. Unwittingly, children are involved, sometimes tragically. Sometimes, too, the war simply enters into their games, and fantasy and reality become merged. A fascinating, linked set of stories brings this to vivid life.

EARLY-MID 20th CENTURY IRELAND

CIVIL WAR *

Dublin 1920 is a dangerous place, full of spies, informants. Sarah Conway cannot figure out just who is telling the truth and who is not. Michael Collins seems to be in charge, but who exactly is on his side?

CIVIL WAR

Set in county Sligo, Katie lives on a farm. Her father, home from the First World War, is suffering from shellshock. Then Katie hears of secrets in the neighbour-hood – secrets to do with war and weapons. What should she do?

JEWISH DUBLIN 1940s *

Hetty lives in 'Little Jerusalem', near the Grand Canal. When she hears of a young refugee hiding out in Dublin, she desperately wants to save her. Can she enlist the help of her Catholic neighbour, Ben?

* FREE Teaching guides available for these books.

See: www@obrien.ie/schools